BY ORDER OF THE
PEAKY
BLINDERS

THE
Shelby
FAMILY

Finn Shelby

John Shelby

Michael Gray

Tommy Shelby

Arthur Shelby

Ada Thorne

Polly Gray

BY ORDER OF THE PEAKY BLINDERS

Introduced by
Steven Knight

With
Matt Allen

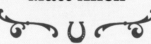

Michael O'Mara Books Limited

With thanks and gratitude to all
the brilliant cast and crew members
who have worked so hard over the
last ten years on *Peaky Blinders*.

Contents

Once Upon a Time in the West Midlands

Introduction by Steven Knight, creator and writer

The real Peaky Blinders, circa 1917

The inspiration for *Peaky Blinders* came from my mother and father. When I was a boy they told me about their own childhoods, growing up in Small Heath, Birmingham. Their stories were like tales from another world, even though I grew up in the same city. Their words came alive in my imagination.

I learned from them that the backstreets of Birmingham in the 1920s were a wild and, in my mind, wonderful place. A lawless, smoky, boozy cast of characters moved to the rhythm of mysterious bangs and booms and hammer blows coming from the car and weapons factories that worked twenty-four hours a day all year round, dropping ash like snow on the blackened streets.

At the age of nine, my mother was a bookies' runner. Local bookies used children to collect bets because off-track betting was illegal at the time and they knew kids wouldn't be suspected and arrested. She carried a basket of washing down Little Green Lane and gamblers dropped their stake, usually a few coins, wrapped in a scrap of paper on which was written the name of the horse they were betting on and their own code name. She carried the dreams and hopes of poor people to the illegal gambling parlour of local bookie Tucker Wright, after stepping around his ferocious dog on a chain, and stepping over the broken beer bottles.

Her father (my grandfather) was one of Tucker Wright's best customers, and often my mother took his only suit to the pawnshop to get money to lay bets. When his horses failed to win he'd play piano and sing in The Garrison pub, in return for free pints and whiskies to allow him to forget how much he had lost.

At the age of nine, my mother was a bookies' runner.

Some tales I was told were just images – almost scenes from a movie. Like when Dad was sent on an errand across Small Heath to take a message to his uncles.

My father's family had worked canal boats, but his uncles were a notorious family of bookmakers and gangsters. My dad was eight and barefoot as he ran across cobbles with a scrap of paper in his hand, given to him by his father to pass on to the uncles. Dad was scared because that family and their associates were also known all across the city as the Peaky Blinders.

Historians may claim the phrase 'Peaky Blinder' went out of use at the turn of the century, but every uncle and auntie

Above: The real Peaky Blinders circa 1920. From left to right: Henry Fowler, Ernest Bayles, Stephen McHickie, Thomas Gilbert. Left: The real Billy Kimber, alongside his character

Dad was scared because that family and their associates were also known all across the city as the Peaky Blinders.

Small Heath circa 1920

in my family and the grandparents told me the term was alive and kicking into the thirties. They were Blinders from their soft woven peaked caps to their shiny black boots. I've consistently found history books to be an unreliable source of information when it comes to working-class history, since mostly people didn't bother to write things down. I trust word of mouth, true memories and, of course, newspaper and court reports.

Dad arrived at a back door in Artillery Street and knocked nervously. The door swung open with a backdraft of cigarette smoke, stale beer and whisky. My dad said he stepped inside to find a group of men slouched in chairs; their flat caps pulled low, razor blades stitched into the peaks, guns only half hidden under open jackets. And in the middle of the group, piled high on a table, was a mountain of silver coins.

This was a neighbourhood where money was scarce, but the Peaky Blinders were kings and princes and this was their treasure. As Dad stared wide-eyed, someone tossed him a half-crown. He said the men were immaculately dressed: every crease as sharp

Football season after football season, I saw the pubs and factories and back-to-backs of Small Heath disappearing.

as the razors in their hats, reflections in their toe caps, dicky bows and ties pulled tight on studded collars.

But what struck my dad most of all was that these men of royal Small Heath blood drank their beer and whisky from jam jars, not glasses. Not a penny of that fortune stashed on the table would be spent on anything so mundane as kitchenware. The money was in the fibre and the leather of their clothes, in their grooming and their guns.

I was around nine years old when Dad first told me that particular story. The image of a gang gathered around their cash stuck with me for decades, I think because each detail was delivered with the wide-eyed world view my father experienced as a kid, living this stuff for real, and for the very first time.

I later had cause to go to Small Heath regularly to watch football and so I saw the last of the old terraces and tenements before they were pulled down. Every pub had a story attached. I'd walk by The Garrison, The Hen and Chickens or The Marquis of Lorne and imagine my grandad banging out a tune on the piano for free beer. I'd picture my mother as a child my age, running through the alleyways with her washing basket in hand.

Most of all, I imagined the Peaky Blinders.

Football season after football season, I saw the pubs and factories and back-to-backs of Small Heath disappearing. It only made me hungrier for the mythology that blew in with the smoke and dust of demolition. There was a pub called The Chain where, in the Peaky days, only women were allowed. Not by legal authority, but because if a man tried to set foot in there he'd be beaten to a pulp by the clientele, who were mostly chain makers from local factories.

The streets teemed with characters. There was a preacher called Jimmy Jesus, who was black and barefoot and who evangelized as he walked the cobbles, pursued by children, for whom Jimmy was the only black man on earth.

There was a man called Tommy Tank who often exploded without warning, destroying whole pubs single-handedly. There were men blinded by war, walking in line with hands on each other's shoulders. There were pubs that opened at 6 a.m. so the factory workers could sink a few pints before reporting to work, where men were paid in beer, washed their machines with beer and apparently lived entirely on beer.

Elsewhere, bare-knuckle boxing matches took place where the loser was tied up and thrown into the canal; he was then required to swim to the nearest lock without the use of his hands. Another man was known to go from pub to pub where he'd then force his head into a cage to fight the rat inside with his teeth. This was mad, wild stuff that most writers wouldn't dare put into a work of fiction because it was too far out, but it was true – all of it. It was our history.

I glimpsed more than most of this disappearing world because Dad grew up to be a blacksmith and farrier. He travelled around the West Midlands shoeing horses. Along with the usual riding stables, he still had connections with various Gypsies and scrap metal dealers who kept yards and horses in the inner-city suburbs and the Black Country. I was the youngest of seven kids and sometimes on a school day he'd say to my brothers and me, 'Do you want to go to school or do you want to come with me?' Of course, the answer was obvious. As a family we'd go to the van to shoe and when we went to the yards I'd meet some incredible characters – they seemed to be from a different universe.

One of the best yards for tea and stories was owned by a scrap metal dealer called Charlie Strong. His helper was a bloke called Curly, and I was later told that Curly was my great uncle. Meanwhile, the yards were like an Aladdin's cave. As a kid, you couldn't help but be fascinated by the junk and jewels to be found there and when I asked if any of the stuff was stolen I was told firmly: 'These people don't steal things. They find things before they're lost.'

Sometimes Dad would take us to Gypsy fairs, such as Stowe Fair, and they were fearsome places full of fearsome characters. He used to be a boxer, so could handle himself pretty well, but I remember when he took me to Stowe, he seemed a little edgy.

There was a man called Tommy Tank who often exploded without warning, destroying whole pubs single-handedly.

He said, 'Son, don't look at anybody. If I get into a fight here, I'll lose.'

He said, 'Son, don't look at anybody. If I get into a fight here, I'll lose.'

Mum and Dad's childhood was set against a supporting cast of war casualties and victims of circumstance. Times were hard and life was often brutal, dangerous and harsh. In summer, mattresses were pulled into the yards and smoked with smudge fires, in order to rid the fabric of bedbugs. Sanitation was almost non-existent. Men fought, women fought back and children sat in the shadows and watched.

Knowing how hard life was didn't ever make the world inhabited by the Peaky Blinders any less appealing to me as a storyteller. I always felt that I'd found my own source of myth and poetry, which I should turn into a narrative that could be shared at some point. Most importantly, the story of these people had never been told. With the help of the BBC, I set about putting that right.

Middle right: *Creator and writer Steven Knight with Cillian Murphy*

PEAKY BLINDERS II
SCENE 1710 SLATE 546 TAKE 3
ROLL A339
DIR Colm McCarthy
D.O.P. Simon Dennis
B+A
DATE 08-06-14

Tommy

PEAKY BLINDERS
ROLL:
369 A
SLATE:
174
TAKE:
1
PANAVISION
A
DIR: Tom Harper
D.O.P. George Steel
13th November 2012

The Creation of
Peaky Blinders

Building the Cathedrals of Light

Twenty-five years ago, creator and writer Steven Knight constructed the working-class fables that would later make up the *Peaky Blinders* story. His idea is quickly brought to life.

STEVEN KNIGHT:

When I thought about dramatizing the stories I'd heard as a kid, I wanted to keep the same mythology; the idea that my parents, as children, had experienced those stories and characters for real. They then passed on the stories to me. I didn't want it to be an exposé of how awful life was in Birmingham back then. I wanted to show people how fantastic, how wild, and how lawless it all was.

In a way, I wanted to approach *Peaky Blinders* in the same style the Americans approached their history on TV. Cowboys were nineteenth-century agricultural labourers, but writers and film-makers had turned their lives into the Wild West. I wanted to maintain an atmosphere on screen where we paid our respects to the lives of British people from that post-First World War era, rather than pitying them. I wanted viewers to imagine the characters in such a way that they looked up to them.

The protagonists poured onto the page. Aunt Polly Gray (Helen McCrory) was a real person and she was terrifying – all the men were scared of her. Arthur (Paul Anderson) was an uncle called Fred. He nailed his wallpaper to the wall because he couldn't be bothered to use glue. There were lots of little character details and fragments that I pieced together to make a far bigger picture.

While I thought it was an amazing period in history, I was in the minority of one. People said, 'Why would you think that 1920s or 1930s Birmingham was the Wild West?' Well, for me

it was. I'd already approached Channel Four with the idea twenty-five years ago. Thank God it didn't happen, because it wouldn't have caught on like it has. Then I got into writing movies (*Dirty Pretty Things, Locke*) and I started to work mostly in LA and Hollywood. But then a golden era of television started and people wanted boxsets and shows of the quality of *The Sopranos*. I was asked if I'd thought about television scripts.

> ## I wanted to show people how fantastic, how wild, and how lawless it all was.
>
> — Steven Knight

'I've got this Peaky Blinders story,' I said …

The person who asked me the question was Caryn Mandabach, from Caryn Mandabach Productions – a force-of-nature producer from Chicago who had worked in American television for years. She was responsible for *Roseanne, 3rd Rock from the Sun* and *Nurse Jackie*, but had become sick of the American system, so she came over to the UK. But she didn't have an office, and alongside another producer called Jamie Glazebrook they used to have their meetings in the Royal Festival Hall on the South Bank in London.

> ## "At the time he wasn't as big a star as he is at the moment, but he's an extraordinary talent. I was honoured."
>
> — Caryn Mandabach

CARYN MANDABACH (EXECUTIVE PRODUCER):

Both Jamie Glazebrook and I were long-term developers at HBO, and while neither of us got any shows on HBO, both of us were very much admiring of what the other was doing. I had just hired Jamie, and the opportunity to do a Steven Knight project – well, we couldn't believe it – it was amazing. At the time he wasn't as big a star as he is at the moment, but he's an extraordinary talent. I was honoured.

I'm in the long-running series business. In the US, when you do the first episode of a show, inside that first episode there are structures that allow the show to grow and last for a long time. Having done a number of very successful returning series, my assumption

Below: *Caryn Mandabach, Executive Producer*

when launching an idea is that we're going to get series two, series three and series four. The audience wants to know character, it doesn't really want to know plot. So our goal with *Peaky Blinders* was to impact as many strands as possible inside that first episode for the viewer to follow.

In talking to Steven initially, we knew the way that he was structuring *Peaky Blinders* would provide the basis for a long-running series. He spoke about Charles Dickens and episodic writing, and characters being at the core of his work. But the most important thing he said was, 'I want to do a show about a damaged guy who can't love and who can't feel when we

first meet him. And I want to follow his journey through the satellites of the characters around him, who are principally his family. Because everyone has a family, everyone has a love interest, and everyone has a business. So he's going to meet people, firstly through his heart being moved by somebody.'

Those were the structures that people watching could follow. When Tommy arrives in Series One and meets Grace, eventually falling for her, you're hooked. You think, 'Hey, that's happened to me! I've felt a bit lonely and miserable and then someone's melted my heart. *Oh, I get it …* ' So no matter who you are, you're connecting with the show in that regard. Or you might connect with the familial aspect: 'Hey, I might not have an Aunt Polly, but I have an important family member in my life.' Or, 'I might not have *those* brothers, but I have brothers. I may not have *that* sister, but I have sisters.' The show built a very relatable construct.

> **" Everyone has a family, everyone has a love interest, and everyone has a business. "**
>
> **– Caryn Mandabach**

We knew because of Steven's language that the first episode would be impacted with all the acorns needed for the show to be full of mighty oaks. We knew it was a long-running series to begin with.

'This is Pretending'

With the help of Caryn Mandabach Productions, the ideas of Peaky Blinders' compelling story are transformed into early scripts.

JAMIE GLAZEBROOK (EXECUTIVE PRODUCER):

When Steven spoke about the show, I saw the whole thing come to life in my imagination. That's a gift Steven just has, but particularly pertaining to this, because it had been in his head for quite a long time. This was a very, very rare case of a TV idea being very fully formed. Every single character, even a character that only had two lines, felt utterly alive and imagined in their internal monologue. It was a perfect fit from that point of view.

STEVEN KNIGHT: I think I had part of a script, but I didn't have a treatment. Thank God for the BBC who, unlike most organizations, if they like an idea often encourage a writer to 'go off and do it'. For me that was heaven. I didn't have to produce any in-depth treatments, or character breakdowns – they just let me get on with it. When it comes to writing the scripts, I just start. What I don't do is make a plan in advance of either the episode or the series. I had an inkling of what it was going to be about, and the period it was going to cover, and started from there.

CILLIAN MURPHY (TOMMY SHELBY): The fact that Tommy was an intelligent working-class Brummie from a working-class family had never been done before. Steven Knight's idea was to mythologize working-class families like the Shelbys, and the characters within their group like Tommy, Arthur and Polly. They do that kind of thing so wonderfully in America, but

not in Britain. Up until then, the British working class of that era had only really been depicted in period dramas such as *Upstairs, Downstairs*. What Steven managed to do was to create a different myth – and it was fascinating. That period between the First and the Second World Wars was not an area that had been investigated in drama so much. The era preceding the First World War and following the Second World War had been covered for sure, but between the two conflicts there was so much going on dramatically, in terms of history and storytelling.

> ## "When Steven spoke about the show, the whole thing came to life."
>
> – Jamie Glazebrook

STEVEN KNIGHT: Beyond that, the first step was to look at some of the things that were going on politically at the time, for plot ideas. But rather than going to the history books, I visited the local newspapers instead, such as the *Birmingham Mail*, searching out real stories. That gave me a much more accurate look at what it was like for ordinary people in the 1920s and 1930s. I think history books often look for patterns, and when a story or happening doesn't fit the pattern it gets forgotten. And there was so much stuff that didn't fit the pattern.

Creator and writer Steven Knight

For example, when I was writing the first series, I discovered a lot of reports in the *Birmingham Mail* of people being arrested for spreading sedition. I remember Dad telling me similar stories. People would go to The Bullring, where somebody would be speaking against the king, or the government. Suddenly the police would appear to take them away. Some of them never reappeared and it was rumoured that the police had them killed. But where was that in the history books? It wasn't just my dad saying it; those stories were in the papers where they featured court reports of people receiving prison sentences of a year or more for sedition. The year was 1919. All the soldiers were returning from France and the authorities were fearful of a revolution.

JAMIE GLAZEBROOK: The world of *Peaky* was fascinating: I remember Steven talking about the pubs as 'cathedrals of light'; the people who had been working in the factories would not stop drinking till the second pint was down. Because of the way that Steven communicates, it was extremely vivid. Also I remember him very early on saying, 'I want the characters to talk fast because in their heads, they're not in a period film; they're in the present.'

Steven once said the words, 'Imagine you're a nine-year-old boy, looking at this world. The men are handsome, the women are beautiful, the horses are shiny, and the cars are glistening.' And we all took that very seriously. It's not gritty at all, it's almost like a fantasy. You'll see every now and then, in these wide shots of Birmingham, a railway line, high up in the air — you're seeing a heightened version of the city.

STEVEN KNIGHT: In terms of writing *Peaky*, as with anything I do, I think about what it's going to be and then I sit down and start. I

write *anything*. I tell myself, 'This isn't the real thing. This is rehearsal. This is pretending.' Then I'll let the writing run and run and run, eventually stopping to read it back, noticing what happens. For the last couple of years, I've been thinking about where it comes from. Sometimes I'll read the work back and have no idea of how I got to the story, or the origins of a particular train of thought.

My writing is absolutely based on real people in real places, speaking in the way they really speak. Some part of me was able to take the memories from my family talking about the Peaky Blinders gang and run it through my imagination. When I write *Peaky* scripts, I'm trying to switch on that memory and let it go, in such a way that it's also like dreaming.

I get so involved in the writing that, when I'm into a script, I can lose sense of what I've been doing. I'll accidentally have two showers in the morning; I've even tried to shave twice, because I'm so involved in the story. I'll look in the mirror and think, 'Shit, I've just done that. *Why am I shaving again?*' Driving when I'm writing a script is quite dangerous …

I had some characters worked out before the writing really started. There was Tommy Shelby: he was the younger brother of the family. Arthur was the older brother and his partner-in-crime. I knew I wanted Ada (Sophie Rundle), his sister, to be there and that she was having an improper relationship with a communist, so I had the communists, too.

Sam Neill's character, Chief Inspector Chester Campbell, was a real person brought from Belfast to control the gangs in Birmingham. (In Series One, he was a chief inspector from the Royal Irish Constabulary installed in Birmingham to find a batch of stolen machine guns taken from the Birmingham Small Arms factory. These guns accidentally fall into the possession of the Peaky Blinders.) I'd learned that, in reality, Campbell had placed flyers around Shankill Road in Belfast, which read: 'If you're over five foot and can fight, you need to join the police.' He recruited a collective as police 'specials' and gave them uniforms and truncheons. Then he let them loose. They were terrifying, but the locals fought back.

> **My writing is absolutely based on real people in real places, speaking in the way they really speak.**
>
> – Steven Knight

Knowing vaguely who the Shelbys were as a family meant I could put a plot together: a hard-nut chief inspector comes over from Ireland to sort out the gangs. Part of his strategy is to place a barmaid called Grace

(Annabelle Wallis) into The Garrison pub as an undercover agent. That was the basis of the story. Once that was in place I got started.

CARYN MANDABACH: I only remember one thing about the early scripts and that was a general feeling. Ben Stephenson (Controller of Drama Commission at the BBC) also only gave one note, and his note echoed our note. Ben said in a sentence:

'Start the story sooner.'

By the way, that's the classic note that all writers get: 'What is the motivation? Start the story sooner ... ' When we gave that comment to Steven, his eyes rolled back in his head. He said, 'Tommy finds some guns.' And that was it. When you give a character like Tommy Shelby a poker hand, you could either give him a good hand or a bad hand. How to play a good hand – *I've found some guns* – is as interesting a way to start a story as having a bad hand. That was Steven's solution and then we never talked about it again. As we read the new scripts we just kept saying, 'Wow, that's fabulous.'

STEVEN KNIGHT: The idea of the stolen guns came during the writing process – they were the catalyst. My mum worked in the Birmingham Small Arms factory (BSA) during the war, putting explosives into shells. The

BSA was often talked about when I was a kid and it was right in the middle of Small Heath. Think about it: a massive factory full of weapons, so what are the gangsters going to do? They're going to steal the weapons.

Plot is best when you don't think logically and you place your characters in a situation: *you've got the Peaky Blinders in the pub; the BSA is based nearby. So where does Ada work? She probably works at the BSA. The BSA has guns. The Peaky Blinders steal some guns. The stolen guns become the plot …*

Allowing the story to develop that way is so much better than working it all out in my head in advance.

PEAKY BLINDERS-SERIES 4
ROLL #A003
SLATE 18
TAKE 1
SCENE 6/42
DIR: DAVID CAFFREY
D.O.P: CATHAL WATTERS I.S.C
DATE: 21st 21 MARCH 2017
A

Shelby Foundation

Fundraising Dinner

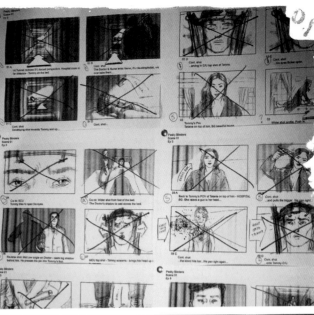

'I Have Plans for the Peaky Blinders'

The key players in the *Peaky Blinders* story are slowly brought together.

STEVEN KNIGHT: I think I had the first episodes written and, in the mysterious way of scripts, I started getting feedback from actors. We hadn't even finished the series, but the scripts were getting out to people. I don't know how that happens. But everybody knows everybody else in the industry, so if something comes along and people think it's good, they start to think, 'Well, I'll get it to my client first.' We got feedback from Cillian Murphy and Sam Neill and we thought, 'Wow, this is great.' And with those two names on board and Helen McCrory too, that attracted the talent. Sam Neill really wanted the part. He told me he was born in Belfast and that he had the accent in his memory. We got lucky with that.

SHAHEEN BAIG (CASTING DIRECTOR): The brilliant thing about the first series was that we had a lot of run-up time into it, which is rare. Normally when you come on to a telly job you have to turn things around quite quickly. I came on board early, so we could take our time and do it properly. Otto Bathurst (director, Series One, episodes one, two and three) was brilliant and open, and he said to me, 'Think of people you wouldn't normally expect to see in these shows and think of this as a movie.' When I cast, I don't differentiate between television and film anyway. I don't change my style. I don't change the actors. I absolutely approached *Peaky Blinders* like it was cinema.

I was ambitious. I tried to think, 'OK, who could you put in this that you maybe wouldn't expect to see in this genre, this world, and period film?' That was challenging because, yes, *Peaky Blinders* is a period piece, but it's very modern. I love reinventing actors and casting actors that people think they've got the measure of and then turning it on its head. That was a joy. I felt like I had a huge amount of freedom.

> **The *Peaky Blinders* script did this brilliant trick of being original, but it also drew from the gangster genre.**
>
> — Cillian Murphy

CILLIAN MURPHY: I first heard about the show in 2011, or something like that. I was aware there was a bit of a revolution happening in television. I was talking to my agent, I was like, 'How come I don't get sent TV scripts – I just get sent films?' And he said, 'Let me have a look.' And then through the agent and some serendipity, these two scripts arrived two years later for *Peaky Blinders*. I read them and knew instantly that it was very special material. I met Steven Knight and Caryn Mandabach, and that's how it came about.

The *Peaky Blinders* script did this brilliant trick of being original, but it also drew from

the gangster genre, the western drama, and the great family crime sagas that we've become familiar with over the years. It managed to borrow from them while making it into something completely original. I felt that when I read the script, the opening sequence in itself was breathtaking on the page (in which Tommy Shelby slowly walks a horse through the cobbled streets of Small Heath and asks a Chinese fortune-teller to blow red dust into its face for good luck).

The beautiful thing about television is it allows a level of investigation and detail that you don't get in a two-hour feature film. As the lead character, to be able to investigate Tommy's state of mind, postwar, over six hours at the beginning was really, really interesting. How he used this combination, or contradiction, of a facility for violence and sensitivity was very interesting, too. Again, the script was borrowing from the tropes of the classic anti-hero, while making it something quite unique.

CARYN MANDABACH: Cillian has a simple standard: 'Is the script great? And can I do something to make this even greater?' That's his only motivation. So his heart is pure, and to find that a pure person responds to a character like Tommy Shelby is very rare. Steven and I met him in a little hotel in South Kensington and he was just stunningly articulate. Both of us had been in the business for some while and we thought, 'Is it us, or is that guy great?' You get a gut feeling when you're in the business long enough and Cillian was very smart and emotionally intelligent. If you're a great actor it doesn't necessarily mean you're emotionally intelligent, or smart. His star quality was underpinned by his obvious acting intelligence.

SHAHEEN BAIG: We didn't reinvent Cillian, he existed and he was already an extraordinary star. But I suppose everybody took a moment to go, 'Cillian Murphy? *Really?*' He's such a very detailed actor. He's forensic almost in the way he approaches things. I suppose we could have put someone in that part who was more obviously dangerous and more obviously a brute, but actually what I thought was fantastic about Cillian was that he's a storyteller – that's what he does so beautifully.

We didn't need the head of that family to be a brute. We didn't need him to be someone who, the minute you looked at him, could break you. It's all about what's going on behind his eyes. I know everyone talks about his eyes, it's slightly clichéd, but what we needed was somebody to head that family who was a beautiful storyteller, who you wanted to go on a journey with. And Cillian had that. He's charismatic, he's secretive, there's a quietness to what he does – you're not getting everything immediately. Even now, at Series Five, we still want to watch him, we still want to go on that journey with him because he's a brilliant storyteller. That's what we wanted and needed for Tommy.

We talked about lots and lots of people. I don't think Cillian had fronted a television show. *Peaky* was the first time, and so it felt like a massive treat to have somebody like him. We didn't have any fatigue from him fronting shows, he felt fresh. We'd got someone who was a movie star and we got someone who put a spin on the character. If you read the first premise of *Peaky Blinders* on a page it's likely you'd think, 'Oh yeah, right, it's that kind of actor …' But then you see Cillian. It was different. The casting of him set out our stall. It said, 'This is the way we're going to approach this piece.' Cillian's casting made everything else so much easier because we didn't have to fall into any predictable potholes.

TOM HARPER (DIRECTOR, SERIES ONE, EPISODES FOUR, FIVE, SIX):
I was interested in the warmer side of Tommy in the script. I was interested in the humanity of people. If you get people doing terrible things, what motivates them? What drives them? That's one of the main things that attracted me to it. What was going to cause those things? It was a murky, morally complex

world – or it can be. Tommy was broken. He was a strong, powerful man who was just broken on the inside and, I guess, repressed. He didn't know how to handle getting in touch with people. It was the same with all the characters, in different ways.

PAUL ANDERSON (ARTHUR SHELBY): It's funny, because when I first saw the script I was more interested in playing Tommy. Otto Bathurst wanted to meet me for Cillian's role. The first thing I was struck by was the fact the character has to speak with a Brummie accent. I said, 'There's no way I can do a Birmingham accent.' So I went along and I met them and we had a cup of tea and that was that: *I'm not going to do a Brummie accent*. It was a positive meeting though; we had a good chat. I was told, 'Look, they've offered the part to Cillian Murphy, but they'd like you for the part of the brother, Arthur.' And I didn't know who that was. When you're given a script and you're told to look at a certain part, really and truly, I only look at the one part. So I wasn't thinking about Arthur. At that point in the script, there were five brothers: Tommy, Arthur, John, Finn and another middle-tier brother, around John's age. I kept thinking, 'Which brother?' I had a reread and I jumped at it. I thought he was great.

Above all else, I identified with Arthur. On a funny level, he was very stuck in his ways. He reminded me of somebody I know and so I got him, I understood him quickly. It was very easy to get into him at first: in Series One, Tommy comes back into his life and wants to control the business again, but Arthur has no time for that because the way things are run suit him just fine.

CARYN MANDABACH: Paul Anderson came through on auditions, as did Joe Cole (John Shelby). We couldn't have been happier and how lucky we were to get Sam Neill, and Annabelle Wallis (Grace Shelby) too.

Before casting, we looked at their work, their plays; we talked to other producers about them. Then we thought of ourselves as audience members. Steven wrote this story and, in every way, you honour what Steven says very carefully, which was: *the women are beautiful, the men are handsome, the horses are big and shiny*. We were definitely going to take him at his word and not mess about, because we're watching television – these people were going to be in our homes.

> **The first thing I was struck by was the fact the character has to speak with a Brummie accent.**
>
> **– Paul Anderson**

TOM HARPER: Of course, there's Polly and there's Tommy and there's Arthur, but then there's always a whole bunch of other interesting people in the story as well: whether that was Arthur Shelby Snr (Tommy Flanagan), or Esme Lee (Aimee-Ffion Edwards), who came in and got married to John Shelby in episode four. There was also Zilpha Lee (Therese Bradley), the Gypsy who agrees to the arranged marriage between John and Esme. So there were all these fascinating characters, strong, powerful characters, both female and male. There was a balance of strength between the male and female that I really liked.

I think Sam Neill revelled in playing the role of Chief Inspector Chester Campbell.

Sam is a real professional and craftsman. He's a class actor, through and through. Because it's a part he had fun with, there was a degree of having an ever so slightly heightened energy. I thought that he pitched it just right. He delivered just enough charisma to the character without blowing it. Chief Inspector Campbell is a real, proper, old-school villain. The danger with those nasty characters is that they can be overdone and then you don't believe them. But he brought just enough to it to make it viciously villainous without stepping over the line into caricature.

SHAHEEN BAIG: Getting the family right was interesting. I think Sophie Rundle happened quite quickly. We saw a bunch of people and she hadn't been in a lot before, but I'd seen her in a couple of things. We did casting sessions, but there was something really sharp about her. She's completely switched on. There was a lot of clarity in what she was doing. Certainly in the first series, there were a lot of men. I wanted to put in women that were strong.

With Helen McCrory, it was an amazing coup to get her, because she is such a ferociously strong actress that you can't take your eyes

off her. When she's in those scenes with Cillian they absolutely match each other. When we got Helen, I thought, 'OK, that's exciting.' Paul Anderson *is* Arthur. For both the brothers – Arthur and John – we saw a fair amount of people. Paul came in and it was a done deal. His spirit struck me, as well as his physicality.

Paul Anderson's really direct; he says what he thinks. What I thought was beautiful in the first series was the journey he took Arthur on. On one hand he could be terrifying, on the other he could be utterly heartbreaking. There was a real melancholy with Paul and, also, he felt very different to Cillian, but they felt like they were part of the same stable. He's an instinctive actor. And that's what we needed for Arthur – a very different energy to Cillian.

Joe Cole is a fantastic young actor and we were lucky to get him when we did. He had a mixture of Tommy and Arthur and there were some similarities to Cillian in style – he could flip. He can turn the mood on its head. Joe can be cold and calculated and also incredibly violent, but there's also a sweetness to him, which we needed because he was the youngest. We wanted to feel like we had three quite different men in Tommy, Arthur and John, but we understood they were part of the same family.

Sam Neill's character was unsettling: he's domineering, but he's also very charismatic. He's charming. Sam can play all the sides of that character. While he's absolutely forensically investigating and analysing a person, Chester Campbell is being charming, so we can understand why Polly gets drawn in during a horrific sexual assault scene in Series Two, because we're drawn in, too.

The thing about *Peaky* is that it's not just about the core cast, it's the supporting roles that make it, too. Like anything you watch, if those other characters don't work, it doesn't matter what the leads are doing. The minute the show starts you've got to be in it and believe that you're in that period in that time, that place.

> ## Sam Neill's character was unsettling: he's domineering, but he's also very charismatic.
>
> – Shaheen Baig

I love that we've got Ian Peck (Curly), a really fantastic actor. The crew that were always there in Charlie's Yard, such as Charlie Strong (Ned Dennehy), these were actors with incredible faces, they were storytellers, all of them. They might come and go in the story, and they might not be there all the time, but they are brilliantly supporting what the main cast are doing.

BENJAMIN ZEPHANIAH (JEREMIAH JESUS):
When Steve wrote the part, he had me in mind. It was odd because, a few months before that, I was talking to a friend from the BBC who works on current affairs about the gangs in Birmingham, the current gangs and the postcode wars that were going on. I said, 'Oh, gangs have been in Birmingham for ages, have you heard of the Peaky Blinders?' She said, 'I've got a book about the Peaky Blinders! Do you want it?' So when I got the part, I called her up and said, 'Did you know about this?' But it was a complete coincidence.

I really liked the character when I read the script. My father was a preacher, so there's a part of me that connected; the preacher bit

"**Casting Benjamin Zephaniah was my nod to Birmingham.**"

– Shaheen Baig

came naturally to me. When I have to give sermons in the show I can go off script easily. There was one scene that didn't make the cut, where I'm preaching in the bar. You see a little bit of it, but most of it was edited out. I had to do some real hellfire preaching. I remember running through it and Cillian turned round and said, 'Shit, I believe you, father.'

SHAHEEN BAIG: In a way, casting Benjamin Zephaniah was my nod to Birmingham. I felt it would be wonderful to have someone in the show who represented the city and that's what he does. I'm from Birmingham, which is why I fell in love with the script because I never get anything set in Birmingham. *Never.* It's ridiculous. And I always wanted to do something set in my own town, so when I got this I thought, 'Oh my Lord, I know all the street references.' It's a very special show for me because it's personal. But then putting ingredients in like Benjamin is just great because he's a hero figure for kids in Birmingham.

'We're on Our Way Up in the World, Brother'

Under the creative eye of directors Otto Bathurst and Tom Harper, *Peaky Blinders* comes to life.

JAMIE GLAZEBROOK: We found that Steve's scripts attracted truly talented people both in front of and behind the camera. Frith Tiplady at our co-production partner, Tiger Aspect, was an astoundingly gifted head of production who joined as an executive producer, relentlessly finding ingenious ways to achieve Steve's vision on camera. We were also joined by the brilliant Greg Brenman from Tiger on Series One and then Will Gould (also at Tiger) on Series Two, Three and Four. To date, each series has had its own producer, starting with Katie Swinden (Series One) who, with our initial directors Otto Bathurst and Tom Harper, made manifest a *Peaky* world so detailed, crafted and immersive, you feel you can smell it.

The character of Tommy Shelby was extraordinary, from the start of Series One. Part of the structure is that you're watching the show, but you're also in the head of this Tommy character, and that's the fascination. He's a very closed-down person in the first episode; he's very cut-off.

CARYN MANDABACH: Otto directed the first three episodes and his choices were so thoughtful. And, by the way, he followed to the letter what Steven wanted; we needed to realize his work in a way that was honouring what he meant. We were reminded that the show should be portrayed as if this was a tale being told to a nine-year-old boy, like you're reading *Lord of the Rings* when you're still a child. Otto slavishly devoted his fierce imagination to honouring the script.

> ## "The interiors must look gorgeous, even though this was a place with nothing."
>
> — Steven Knight

STEVEN KNIGHT: The conversations I had with the crew were always around mythologizing the people and places. I'd say, 'Don't think of this as a typical British working-class drama – everyone should be good-looking, everyone should be dressed immaculately; the interiors must look gorgeous, even though this was a place with nothing.' And I wanted to mix the history of my grandfather, my dad's dad. On the other side they were Gypsies. There was this mix of part Gypsy, part canal-boat people. So we had to have the rural, edge-of-town sensibility about it as well, with the horses and the blacksmiths …

JAMIE GLAZEBROOK: Working on every aspect of the very complicated matter of making a TV show, with an incredible cast and scripts but with limited time and money, can be tricky. The extraordinary crew found creative solutions to problems. I think that's part of the magic; a lot of the time, you're imagining so much more than you're actually seeing. Mostly that's down to Steven's writing, because it conjures up so much. But, also, there was very, very judicious and clever film-making.

TOM HARPER: We were getting script pages, sometimes on the same day we were shooting the scenes involved. We could have been in real trouble but, fortunately, the cast and crew were so good that we often turned up on the day and worked out what we were doing. But that's a mark of quality in the pages and the cast and crew that we had. It was also quite liberating in a way, because you can't really prep. You get the pages and you do what you can, so it means you have to be spontaneous and very responsive. That's scary, but it's exciting as well.

JAMIE GLAZEBROOK: One early example of this in the first series was where the Peaky guys were spread out at one end of Garrison Lane, and Billy Kimber (Charlie Creed-Miles) and his men were at the other in the series finale. They're clearly headed for a gunfight. In the original script the plan was for a huge battle, with people going into The Garrison and bullets flying through the glass. It was a full-on action scene, the OK Corral, but we didn't quite feel we could mount it properly. We asked Steven to think of something else and came up with the extraordinary image of two gangs lining up in the street, with Ada in black, pushing her pram between the two groups.

Suddenly that was a far more powerful image; it brought you back to the war. The director, Tom Harper, played that Sergio Leone trick where he made the build-up so exciting. It was incredible, from the moment where Tommy talks about 'The Soldier's Minute'. You see the little kid running along Garrison Lane, and from there it builds and builds.

STEVEN KNIGHT: When it came to the look of the show, the fashion, there were all the people I knew as a kid, and the idea of the series was to mix their look with the Gypsy style. It's the same with the people working on the canals and canal boats and there's a certain art to the clothing: the waistcoats, the roses, elephants and all those special designs. I wanted to keep that along with the urban gangster style. The mixture of those two was essential in making the look. Part Gypsy, part canal-boat people.

Some of it was based on reality. In the First World War, British troops and Australian troops had their hair shaved, because nits congregated around the nape of the neck. They didn't want to be completely shaved, so they cut the back and sides of the skull, leaving the hair on top. When they came back from the war, that's what they looked like. Some people moved on and grew their hair out. Others carried on with it. There were police mugshots from the time and the men usually had those cuts.

The clothes were fantastic. They were heavy and well constructed; the suits were tailored and handmade, and the clothes always matched. The men took a real care in how they looked. We're used to women taking that much care in their appearance, but these men were dandies. The gangsters were dandies; in London and in all the big cities, such as Glasgow, you knew who the gangsters were because of the way they dressed, and they dressed well. It was the same in America.

I think part of that attitude came from the military. People were made to wear uniforms but when they'd got back from the fighting they thought, 'Fuck that, I'm going to wear whatever I want, I'm going to look the business.' The other reason was that the people in Birmingham during that time lived in a very poor environment. They had no control over anything except for what they were wearing. So they used to spend a lot of money on clothes. That gave us a real opportunity in the look of the show – I went back to the mythology idea and decided that everybody had to look fantastic, because we'd got a bit of permission from reality.

Peaky Blinders coincidentally chimed with the zeitgeist of what was actually going on in fashion, and then began to affect it. There was a trend where men were becoming more dandy; women tended to like men wearing those clothes. The look caught on again. I was even sent a photo of a Swedish football team travelling to an away game. The whole squad had the suits and the flat caps; the manager was dressed as Alfie Solomons (Tom Hardy). In New York, people are dressing like it; in Santa Monica, California. I went into a bar in Turkey and saw three blokes dressed like Peaky Blinders. It was great.

CARYN MANDABACH: Fashion follows TV. I'm not a cowboy, but I wear cowboy boots and I wear a bandana around my neck. When you're mythologizing, you're going to focus on the clothes. Those hats had meaning and they were wearing them for a lot of reasons, including violence, because there were razor blades stitched inside the peaks. John F. Kennedy didn't wear a hat to his inauguration in 1961 and then nobody wore hats again – the impact was huge. Prior to JFK everybody wore hats, so I wasn't the least bit surprised that people copied the look.

JAMIE GLAZEBROOK: Otto hadn't told us that we were going to be listening to Nick Cave for the opening credits of the show. But it was always in our minds that *Peaky Blinders* couldn't be like a stodgy period drama. The music was perfect. All of us had huge grins spread on our faces, because it was exactly the world and the state of mind that Steven was thinking about.

The theme music, especially Nick Cave & The Bad Seeds' 'Red Right Hand', managed to evoke what Cillian called an 'outlaw feel' to the music; you realize you're watching something with the grain of a spaghetti western. That sort of swagger was really important to us. We've used music as a way into the characters' heads. It's never there to give an episode the injection of energy. It's the internal monologue of the characters.

I love the fact that it shakes you out of thinking that it's distant, that it's a period drama. It makes everything feel more present.

SHAHEEN BAIG: The first time I realized how special it was going to be was the read-through for episode one. But at that first session, Otto made me read-in, because sometimes you don't have a completely full cast at a read-through and there's the odd character that needs to be played. So I had to read the first line of the dialogue. I looked around the table and, of course, all these extraordinary people were there. I've never been more nervous. *Cheers, Otto, thanks for that.* When I heard them read, I thought we were making something special.

Then when I saw the first episode with Nick Cave & The Bad Seeds combined with the action, it was extraordinary. I think the music is another character in *Peaky Blinders* and it's an important one, and it has continued to be throughout the series. I felt like I was watching a piece of really ambitious television.

CARYN MANDABACH: At first, *Peaky Blinders* was a failure! Check the ratings – nobody watched! Some viewers didn't think it was for them, they thought it was for someone else, because they didn't watch BBC2. They thought it was too esoteric.

We edged up because of the nascent iPlayer; we were lucky to happen at the same time. It spread through word of mouth. Thank God for the British people yakking away – and that's the truth. So we were not a hit, but we felt honoured by the people who did love us. I think it really wasn't until Series Three that we saw a turning point. And 100 per cent credit has to go to the BBC for sticking with it.

Part One

The Boss

Cillian Murphy on Tommy Shelby

Who is Tommy Shelby? It's one of the big questions of *Peaky Blinders*.

For an actor, he is such a fertile character. The fact that this man was formed by his experiences in the First World War has been the driving theme behind the show. His generation – a lot of those boys, really, like his brothers Arthur and John, and his friend Danny Whizz-Bang (Samuel Edward-Cook) – went out to a horrific war and, when they came back, they were completely different. The experiences of conflict have created a duality in Tommy that we see when we first meet him, from the beginning of Series One: he's clearly highly intelligent; he's a decorated soldier, so he's been courageous; but then he's emotionally fractured, suffering with what was then called shell shock, but is now known as post-traumatic stress disorder (PTSD). There was so much material to dig into – it's a gift of a part.

To prepare for the role, I did a lot of research into the impact PTSD had on soldiers in the First World War – I did a lot of reading. As everyone now knows, the soldiers returning from the horrors didn't receive a lot of help or support. Men who suffered from shell shock were regarded by some people as cowards; there was no therapy, there was no understanding of the damage they'd experienced, and they were just spat back into society and told to get on with their lives. It's terrifying when you think about it now but, as we know, the horrors of war that existed then still exist today, though the stuff men like Tommy Shelby experienced and witnessed, I couldn't even begin to conceptualize. Trying to put all of that into a character, mixing it round, and making something fresh with it was so stimulating.

In this period, between the wars, Tommy Shelby has an incredible journey, rising from a working-class family as an ambitious gangster before becoming an Officer of the British Empire, Tommy Shelby OBE, and the Labour MP for Birmingham. But this path, and his emotions and ideas throughout, have been formed by the First World War. I think it gave him a huge disdain for the Establishment, for authority and for the aristocracy; for the officer class, for the cavalry; and even for religion. It also took away any fear of death he may have had prior to that conflict – or the fear that normal people have, anyway. I think his postwar attitude, combined with a relentless brand of resourcefulness and intellect, has turned him into an arrow, in terms of capitalism and ambition. I think he's completely fearless. That makes him an unbelievable strategist and a very dangerous foe. I think his mood was set as: 'I'm going to get everything now and fast, because I'm not afraid to die. And if I die tomorrow, that's fine, but for as long as I'm left alive, I'm just going to take it.'

Later, as the show moves out of Series Four and into Series

I'm not a traitor to my class. I am just an extreme example of what a working man can achieve.

Tommy Shelby

Five, Tommy's circle becomes closed in terms of the values that he may have had as a younger man. There are hints: he certainly held socialist values and was perhaps a member of the Communist Party. I think these values, despite his best efforts, are slowly coming back to life again. Nobody could deny that, many times, what he's been involved in and the way he's carried out things – the violence, the killing – have been horrendous, but there are good core values there and they have been dormant. As his story progresses (as he sets up the Shelby Foundation and becomes a Member of Parliament), I think some light is shed on them again.

War even affects the way he reacts as a father, later on in the story. It goes back to his experiences before the war and how the world was before he saw a lot of terrible death and destruction, and the pointlessness of war. I suppose it's the idea of trying to preserve that innocence in children, which we all experience as parents but, for Tommy, because of what he's been through, it's magnified. And because of the world he moves in, his children are a target. *Always*. He has the thing of loving his children, wanting to bring them up and getting them safely to adulthood but then, if you're somebody like Tommy Shelby, they're always going to be marked. It's just a constant state of anxiety for him.

It's through his relationships that we see moments of light. When he meets Grace Burgess in Series One, he softens a little. But then it's revealed she's working against him as an undercover member of the police, for Chief Inspector Chester Campbell. This betrayal sets him back. When they are later reconciled in the story and marry, we definitely see another softening of Tommy, but we also see the same thing during his relationship with the Shelbys. Even though his relationship with the greater family is complex and incredibly fraught and full of tension – as it is with Arthur, Polly and Ada – I think he would lay his life on the line for all of them. Grace is the beginning of our seeing all of that in his character.

There are setbacks for Tommy along the way but, throughout the story, it always feels to me as if, very, very slowly, he's making

I know that you all want me to say to you I'll change, that this fucking business will change, but I've learned something in the last few days … Politicians, fucking judges, lords and ladies. They're worse than us, and they will never admit us to their palaces, no matter how legitimate we become, because of who we are.

Tommy Shelby

progress towards becoming something more resembling a balanced human persona.

Having spent four years fighting during the Great War, the only form of expression that delivered results, to Tommy Shelby's mind, was violence. And obviously he excelled at it. We see violence on the street today and we're shocked and we're shaken, but in the 1920s and 1930s, I think it was commonplace. What's interesting about Steve Knight's writing is that when the violence happens, there are always consequences. If someone gets badly beaten up, like Tommy does at the hands of Father John Hughes (Paddy Considine) in Series Three, they go to hospital and they're in there for a significant period of time. If an Italian Mob member is killed, then the Mob comes after the killers later on, and there's a vendetta, as in Series Four. It's a massive price to pay.

I say all these things with the caveat of it being a gangster show. I don't think Steve's ambition is to make the violence sexy or to glamorize it: it's ugly and messy. People are dying and getting injured. People are broken by violence. So I think Tommy is aware of how effective violence is in terms of a tool to keep his adversaries down and to intimidate, and to keep power. But it's not something he enjoys.

For a while, he also craves true legitimacy in a business sense, until he eventually realizes in Series Three that members of the Establishment are no better than the Peaky Blinders, in terms of their values and beliefs. I think that's why he then moves so effortlessly into politics, because corruption is very familiar to him. He thinks, 'I understand this, I understand this world,' and I think he becomes more at ease with the fact that he is the outsider, the gangster. He stops trying to hide his true self.

It's a part of the character that's been interesting for me, because that's the classic gangster narrative. The idea a person can start off on the mean streets of Birmingham, or wherever it may be, before becoming legitimate. Then there's usually a fall from grace. I think with Tommy it's a slightly different arc he's going through. He thinks, 'OK, now I'll keep one foot in this world, this legitimate world of power, but I can also keep one foot in the other.' And through that he begins to wonder whether the core beliefs he had as a much younger man, the socialist values, weren't so mistaken after all.

Aside from his relationship with Polly and his marriage to Grace, Tommy's attitude towards women seems transactional a lot of the time. Certainly, the physical aspects of it are usually transactional, as with horse trainer and rich widow, May Carleton (Charlotte Riley), in Series Two. (Tommy is still grieving over Grace's betrayal.) But, at the same time, he's never ever, ever violent towards women, and I think for him it's not a conscious plan: 'I treat women equally.' It's just an idea of, 'I want whoever is best for the job, I don't care whether they're men or women.' I think without him knowing it, he's almost a prototype feminist. Gender is completely immaterial to him; when it comes to getting something done he picks the best person, and that's why there are a lot of women around him. I also think that, because of his psychological state, it takes him a long time to be able to connect with women in a meaningful way, emotionally.

He's transactional in a lot of his relationships, though. When he messes up with the Russians in Series Three and allows the police to take away Arthur, Polly and some of the other Shelbys,

A good man needs to hold out sometimes.

Tommy Shelby

Tommy is even ruthless with his own family. I think he has a sort of cognitive dissonance in those situations. He can say to the people he cares for, 'Look, I can love you, but I will still manipulate you in a strategic way. That shouldn't affect the way we look at each other, obviously you're my family and I love you, but … *I am going to use you.*' For some reason, he's able to compartmentalize it so that love and illegal business strategy can coexist quite easily.

Often, when I'm playing the character and doing those scenes, I think, 'Well, there's three interpretations of this. There's one where he's acting out of the goodness of his heart because he loves this person. Or he's doing it because he wants to get something from this person. Or he's doing it for both of those reasons simultaneously.' It's fascinating and people can interpret that in the same way. They can say, 'Oh, he's just a bastard, using his family.' Or, 'He loves his family and he wants the best for them.' Or, 'He's both.' It's so much fun to play with and there's no correct interpretation: it's whatever the audience decides to interpret, or how they decide to interpret it. I imagine if you watched *Peaky Blinders* in one go, you'd have one interpretation. Or, if you watched each series as it aired you might have another. That's the beauty of long-form television, it can shift depending on how you consume it.

Within the story there is a complex fabric of female characters that shape how Tommy acts, or reacts. There's Grace, Lizzie, his sister Ada – all of them are strong women moving within his orbit. Polly Gray, his aunt, is, I think, Tommy's closest ally. She's the most trusted member of the family in his eyes, both because of her intellect and also her connection to the Gypsy Romany culture, which Tommy's also still strongly connected to. She can read him like nobody else can; that's her strength, but they have a weird relationship. She's his aunt, but sometimes it's more like a brother–sister relationship. At other times it's like a mother–son relationship. On occasions, it's like a husband and wife relationship. There are elements of all of those relationships in it.

I think it's my favourite in the show, because it is so complicated and convoluted, and it's never settled. It's always shifting and that I find brilliant to play with. Then, of course, I just adore acting with Helen McCrory. She's one of my favourite actors. I think that the relationship with Polly and Tommy is key to the show's success.

When his relationships are badly affected, the progress that Tommy makes towards becoming more balanced and human is set back. Grace's death in Series Three is one example. He's feeling pain but he can't handle having access to all that emotion. He's grieving, but in a way where he doesn't express his feelings and it comes out in self-imposed isolation, or rage. All those things are dramatically interesting. I think that's why

the audience are so fascinated with the gangsters' familial code. People of that type behave in a very heightened way. Sometimes we watch those extreme reactions and think, 'God, I'd love to be able to do that!' Or, 'I'd love to express myself like that, or just act out like that.' It's very appealing: the extreme reactions where everything's turned up very, very high.

The reason why relationships like the one between Polly and Tommy work so well, and also his relationships with Arthur and Ada, is because the writing is some of the best you'll find on TV in the world. Steve is a writer at the peak of his powers. He once said to me that the story and the dialogue come out of him like a spring of water. It's the same with the characters he constructs, because he's from Birmingham, because he's heard these stories growing up, and because playing with those mythologies is not a chore. It's a joy for him. We're very lucky to have a writer who, as of now, has written those thirty hours of television.

When it came to shaping the character of Tommy, I think at the beginning there was more of a dialogue between the two of us. From what I've gleaned, Steve writes for the actor. He knows the way I am and the way I interpret the character, so he writes for that. But because it is so beautifully written, I never want to change anything. We discuss things. We discuss the journey, we discuss the story arc, but these scripts come to me in advance and, whenever I see them, I just couldn't be more grateful.

The Blunt Instrument

Paul Anderson on Arthur Shelby

Let's not misunderstand what Arthur Shelby is. He is a mad dog, happiest when he's at Tommy's side protecting his brother and the rest of the family. Arthur loves that role.

But there's so much more to him than that. In reality, he's a very tortured soul, affected by the horrors of the First World War and everything he's seen on the battlefield. I say this because it's not very interesting for an actor to simply portray a very dangerous man, an evil man, a violent man. It's fun, but it's not compelling. Arthur is involved in great fight scenes, his rage is incredible, but from an emotional and dramatic context that's not enough for me. I don't think there's anything good about playing a violent man just because he can be violent. And Arthur Shelby is so much more than that.

He is vulnerable and lost; he is affected by the violence inflicted upon him by his country during political conflict. (So is Tommy – he's just as fucked up as Arthur in his own way.) Steven wrote Arthur as a character that had brought back a series of psychological issues from the battlefield and I've tried very hard to bring those issues out on screen. Arthur has an addictive personality, for example. He's a complete addict and he loves drink – and cocaine, once he's introduced to 'Tokyo' in Series Two. I think in one series he was never without drugs. I had even told the director, 'Listen, I want to be taking cocaine in every scene. Every chance I get, I want him to be using the drug.' I wanted to show that men like Arthur self-medicated to shut out the nightmarish experiences of being former soldiers. He was getting high to soothe the shell shock, because that's what people really did in those days: they drank, they fought, they fucked to forget.

After five series of *Peaky Blinders*, I know Arthur so well and I understand his weak spots, and – believe it or not – one of his biggest vulnerabilities is love. His love for Tommy is huge; his love for the whole family is huge, but as we see throughout the *Peaky Blinders* story, love, loyalty and trust can be abused. When Arthur feels cheated in that respect, he often goes off the rails.

In Series One his father, Arthur Shelby Snr, shows up and sells him a dream story that he plans on moving to America in order to open 'The Shelby Casino', with Arthur alongside him. 'I've seen the name above the door!' he tells his son. He then uses Arthur to steal money from the family in an act that eventually culminates in heartbreak. The love Arthur has for his dad is never reciprocated – Arthur Shelby Snr only shows Arthur love to cheat his family out of money – and he later abandons his devotion.

When Arthur eventually finds Arthur Shelby Snr fleeing Birmingham on the train station platform, he realizes his father

Tell your boss what you saw here today. Tell him you don't fuck with the Peaky Blinders.

Arthur Shelby

had no intention of taking him to America; there wasn't even a casino. But Arthur had believed every word his father had said, because he'd gone back to being a ten-year-old boy again, acting as if his dad was taking him to the zoo. *He was innocent.* But Arthur Shelby Snr reverted to type – he let his family down, he abused the trust, and abandoned Arthur. This causes Arthur an immense amount of pain and he then tries to kill himself in the boxing club, but his poorly made noose snaps as he thrashes around in its grip.

Tommy abuses his trust, too; he takes advantage of Arthur under the excuse that it's for the greater good, such as when he turns the family over to the police at the end of Series Three. In Series Two, Polly even accuses Tommy of neglecting his brother's mental health because he'd rather have 'a mad dog' at his side than somebody slow; a soldier moving more ponderously under the effects of opium and bromide, which Arthur takes to ease his mental trauma. Cillian and I discussed this recently. We reckon that Tommy doesn't want any harm to befall the Shelby family, but he does use us for his ambitious desires, if necessary.

Whenever I talk about the show, sometimes there's Arthur speaking, and then there's the way I think outside of Arthur. I step outside of Arthur and I have my own thoughts. Outside of the characters, Cillian and I have both realized that we've been doing this for several years, playing these personalities, and I believe deeply that when we put those costumes on, Cillian and myself *are* Arthur and Tommy. We feel like brothers. I look at Cillian, but I don't see Cillian, I see Tommy; Cillian looks at me and sees Arthur, not Paul.

I have this love for Tommy. A brotherly, deep-rooted affection. In character, even as a joke, and even when we're not on camera, I'll spring to his defence, just for fun. If a member of the production crew, or a fan, comes on set and tries to get close to Tommy, I'll be the one stepping in to protect him. It's become natural for me, an Arthur-like reaction. I certainly don't act in those moments.

But that love extends beyond Tommy. When John dies in Series Four and when we later see him on his deathbed, I didn't need to act in those scenes. The feelings I experienced were true, and very close to the stuff Arthur would have been experiencing. Seeing John like that, having been shot by the Changrettas, was like watching something happen to my real brother. Obviously, I don't live in that criminal world and God forbid anything like that happened to my brother in real life, but I certainly didn't need to draw upon any imagined emotional reserves while I was acting. The emotions I felt, the feelings I had, were real – all of them. Joe Cole leaving the show was like losing my brother. There was no surprise in the sadness I had that morning.

The most important weakness that Arthur possesses is his wife, Linda (Kate Phillips). She has changed him; she's a chink in his armour. People often say, 'Well, wait a minute, wouldn't it be nice to see Arthur married and living on a farm with chickens…' It's even whispered, around Series Three, that Arthur is set to move to California with Linda to set up a convenience store, in order to escape the criminal life. The only thing that would make Arthur do something like that is Linda.

In the same way that Superman disguised himself as Clark Kent, so Linda gives Arthur an alter ego. She tames him, but it stops him from being himself. She dresses him up in country attire. He plays at being a father. He plays at being a country gent. He even grows out his Peaky haircut. But that's not him; he's not being true to himself. Arthur is pretending. And that's dangerous, given his personality.

I imagine that every night during that time he'd be there in that country house, a glass of whisky in his hand, a revolver in his

lap. We might have even filmed a scene like that, where he sits in a big chair, reminiscing about the Peaky Blinders days and longing for the violence. But more than the violence, Arthur longs for the life. He craves the camaraderie, the fraternity, the brotherhood of John and Tommy and The Garrison Tavern. If you were to speak to any gangster, or anyone involved in that kind of villainy, the most important thing to them – *the juice* – is the life. It's not crime. It's not violence. Their juice is the way of life. That's what Arthur misses, because Linda took that from him.

Linda's pious ways also screw with his head, big time. She's religious and she forces her faith and ideals upon him. The Bible gives him a belief in God – he feels that something, or someone is protecting him and guiding him – but I don't think it's really Catholicism or Christianity. It's something else. But anyone on the edge, like Arthur is, will jump on a breadcrumb of hope: something that offers salvation, or a respite from the noises in his head. If you offer him religion with the promise, 'This is going to take away some of those demons. This is going to silence the noises in your mind,' he's going to buy into that idea, desperate for any relief.

That day in the war when Tommy, Arthur and the others nearly die, and we sing 'In the Bleak Midwinter' with the preacher Jeremiah Jesus – that wasn't an act of God. Arthur and Tommy both agree on that. But from thereon, as they say, in Series Four, the Shelby brothers live life to the full because simply being alive is a gift to them – they got away with it in France. Arthur's brief acceptance of God was all for Linda, nothing else.

Tommy and John take digs at Arthur and his religious beliefs. They make comments about the way Linda has softened him. On the surface he seems to take it with a pinch of salt, he cops it on the chin because John, especially, has always been that way with him; the battle between those two has been based in humour and mockery. But later he will have sat there and taken a look at himself. Arthur would have thought, 'What am I doing?

I am emotional.
I just don't know
what fucking
emotion it is.

Arthur Shelby

Why I am praying to this? Why am I putting hope in this religious idea? Why haven't I got a bottle of whisky in my hand? Why haven't I got a gun by my side?' Because essentially, a person with a bottle of whisky and a revolver is who Arthur is. That's the man you're dealing with.

What Linda leaves afterwards is a vulnerable man. Arthur becomes slow and puffy. If Luca Changretta (Adrien Brody) and his men had attacked Arthur at the cottage in Series Four, they would have got to him like they got to John and Michael. Had they reached Arthur at that point, it would have been open season: he was weak, open, exposed to attack. I doubt he would have survived. He would have ended up dead.

Arthur doesn't share the same ambition as Tommy – they're different animals. When Tommy takes control of the Shelby business at the start of Series One, Arthur has no time for that. The style in which the Shelby family are running things suits him just fine. Arthur's really not interested in the grand plans Tommy harbours. He's not interested in running race meetings, he's interested in running the streets of Birmingham – the pubs, the racketeering, the protection scams. That's going nicely for him. Tommy's schemes don't bother him.

But Tommy's manoeuvres cause Arthur to struggle. As the elder brother, he should be more in control; it's Arthur that should be telling Tommy what to do, not the other way around. From an ego point of view, it's a hard one for Arthur to swallow. It's very troublesome for his younger brother to come along and almost make him look the fool. We all know that Arthur has an element of vulnerability. That vulnerability makes him prone to ridicule in some instances. He can be bullish in others. And he's not always very bright, let's put it that way.

The classic example of his state of mind arrives when it's revealed that Arthur is the last to know about the stolen guns from the Birmingham Small Arms factory in Series One. That soon becomes a continuing theme throughout the show. Maybe that's for the best in some cases. He's always putting his foot in his mouth. Steven hasn't written him to be a complete idiot, but he can make mistakes.

He has a big mouth, as seen in Series One when he reveals to Grace in The Garrison Tavern that Danny Whizz-Bang isn't really dead. She puts two and two together that Danny's grave is a ruse – it's where the stolen guns have been stashed. But Steven doesn't want Arthur to be dim, so when he's calculated and when he does want to be as shrewd as Tommy, he's capable. But there are times when one would think that Arthur isn't very clever. In actual fact, he can be.

Arthur doesn't see his own qualities, but other people do. Maybe it's me, as who I am – I don't identify with his qualities – but so many people say to me, 'We love Arthur, we care about Arthur, we hope he's going to be all right.' I think that's because people can see he's open; his heart is on his sleeve. *He is who he is.* He doesn't pretend, he's not lying. What you see is what you get with him, and I think people like that in a character. I know I do. I don't want to be fucked around by someone wearing a mask, a person who lies all the time. I want someone in my life, a friend, who's very open and candid, and that's what Arthur is.

Arthur hasn't got any time for women. I put that very simply, as very un-PC and as misogynistic as it might be, but that was the world he lived in. There's Linda, his wife. Maybe his aunt Polly is the only other woman who has any effect or bearing on his thinking. But other than that, Arthur has no emotion towards women. None whatsoever. As for Lizzie Stark (Natasha O'Keeffe), Esme (Aimée Ffion-Edwards) and the women that Tommy encounters – May Carleton, for example – Arthur doesn't view them as anything. They're just sexual objects, whereas Tommy views most of his relationships with them as transactional.

It's hard for me to tell which scenes have best defined him because I haven't seen the show. I know that sounds weird, but I haven't watched *Peaky Blinders*, because I've read it a million times. I've played the scenes in my head. I know the story back to front, so I don't need to sit there when it airs and watch it that way. For me, it's some of the small things that define him. The scene with John on his deathbed, for example. In Series Two, I beat a kid to death in a boxing match. I see red, I knock him down, I knock him out, but I don't stop. I carry on beating him and I kill him. He was only twenty years old, and later I feel terrible for it. When the kid's mother comes to me in the pub, she tries to shoot me, saying, 'Somebody has got to stop you people.' I remember that day. I remember that scene and it was a moving moment for me – there was a lot of emotion.

Point that thing at my head – that's where the trouble is.

Arthur Shelby

I also feel that the scene when Arthur kills Vincent Changretta (Kenneth Colley) in Series Three, was important to the development of his character. The Mafia man had ordered the killing of Grace, and if you ask Cillian what Tommy's weakness is, it's one thing: Grace. And Tommy was about to go Jack the Ripper on Changretta. He pulls out a toolkit of torture, full of scalpels and razor blades. His plan is to slice him up for what he's done to us. But Arthur sees a flicker in Tommy, a sign that it wasn't really him and that he didn't want to do it.

Meanwhile, Changretta was an old man, an old villain who gave orders. It was his sons who were at fault. Don't get me wrong; Vincent Changretta lived by the sword, so he had to die by it, but Arthur wants to free Tommy of the blood on his hands. He puts him, and Changretta, out of their miseries by firing a bullet at the old man's head, because Tommy was going to make

it slow and very, very painful. But ultimately it would have been painful for them both. My swift killing could be viewed as mercy.

I always go on set realizing how very lucky I am. A lot of people say this when they work with good writers and directors, but it's not all the time that this happens. When you're given gifts of scenes and lines it's incredible. And some of the stuff that happens in *Peaky Blinders* has been fantastic. I say this about all the actors in the show – Cillian, Finn Cole, Joe Cole, straight through the cast, Helen McCrory – the stuff that Steven is writing is a gift for us all to play. It's great. I put that moustache on, I wear those clothes, and I transform. It is a ball to play Arthur and I don't struggle to get into him.

But sometimes I struggle to get out. I find it hard to leave Arthur behind, I really do. It's all work as far as I'm concerned, regardless of the methods or the approach I take to acting. When I'm shooting *Peaky Blinders*, when I go home at night to my girlfriend, it still informs what I'm doing. When I'm out of filming, I can slowly switch off and become Paul again. Once filming has finished for the series there's a slow decompression process I go through where I completely shed Arthur until the next time.

But, during filming, I revel in him. I revel in being him and I revel in playing him. He's hard to let go of sometimes.

A Soldier's Minute

Meet the *Peaky Blinders*: a family drama big on love, loyalty and bloody violence.

An Insider's Look at Series One

Through The Garrison Tavern's smoky saloon-bar doors and onto the filthy, choking streets of Birmingham; past the fire-belching factories and along the canals and away to the horse fairs and Gypsy caravan sites, *Peaky Blinders* exploded onto BBC2 in September 2013. Its stories were underpinned by political corruption and gangland scheming; factory strikes and familial power. A list of dead men lost to the mud and barbed wire of the First World War battlefields only enhanced a creeping sense of desolation. Directed by Otto Bathurst and Tom Harper, and featuring a cast that included Cillian Murphy, Helen McCrory, Paul Anderson, Sophie Rundle, Sam Neill and Joe Cole, *Peaky Blinders*' pacey dialogue and tightly woven character trajectories slowly but surely established a high benchmark for future British dramas.

The plot was both compelling and complex. Set in 1919, a crate of machine guns and ammo, taken from the Birmingham Small Arms munitions factory, have fallen into the hands of a criminal enterprise run by the Shelby family – known in the city as the Peaky Blinders. The happening was a fictitious stroke of good fortune; the story rooted in historical events.

'I realized it was such an interesting time,' said Steven Knight,' because the men had gone away to war and the women had done their jobs in their absence. At the same time the suffragette movement had come in. When the men came back, the women were different. But the men were different, too, because they had been traumatized, and the women had been doing the work in their absence. Then laws were passed which prioritized jobs for men.'

> **The one minute: The Soldier's Minute. In a battle, that's all you get. One minute of everything at once. And anything before is nothing. Everything after, nothing. Nothing compared to that one minute.**
>
> **– Tommy Shelby**

With the guns stashed away, the gang, led by the calculating Tommy Shelby – a decorated soldier impacted by the traumas of conflict and haunted with night terrors – engage in a race to shift the merchandise. In their slipstream are the police, driven by the heavy-handed leadership of Chief Inspector Chester Campbell, an Irish official controlled by the command of Winston Churchill. An undercover agent, Grace Burgess, is planted into the Peaky Blinders' pub, The Garrison Tavern, as barmaid. But the IRA have also discovered the weaponry is in the Peaky Blinders' possession and attempt to make a trade, either through a financial or violent exchange.

> **Everyone's a whore, Grace. We just sell different parts of ourselves.**
>
> **— Tommy Shelby**

Meet the Shelbys

Onto this stage arrived a series of instantly memorable characters. Crime boss Tommy is a man with grand ambitions; he hopes to expand the Shelby's illegitimate gambling business beyond the hinterlands of Small Heath, Birmingham. His older brother, Arthur, once a senior head of the gang, becomes increasingly violent and unpredictable. Authority has been wrestled from him following his emotional struggles in the fallout of combat, and he's soon nudged to one side by Tommy's underhand scheming. Meanwhile, John Shelby is the youngest foot soldier in the Peaky Blinders gang, an aggressive force capable of delivering violence to further the family's ambitions, often with the use of the razors stitched into the brim of his flat cap.

The women of the family are equally as fearsome, however. The matriarch, Polly Gray, aunt to the Shelby boys and a character capable of striking anxiety into her nephews, is Tommy's only equal within the company. During The Great War, she ran the Shelby business as it traded in illegal off-track betting. When the men returned, the power was taken away from her.

'She was running the book, doing the gambling,' says Steven Knight. 'There would have been a couple of men around to enforce her work but, basically, women like Polly trusted that the men were coming back and the word was, when they did, the people around her better not have fucked up.'

Polly's attitude has been hardened by circumstance. It's revealed through the first two series that she was deemed unfit to be a parent and watched, helplessly, as nuns took her two children away in an act of sadistic social care. 'That brutalizes Polly,' says Helen McCrory. But her character is both intimidating and gentle-hearted: on camera, the familial relationship of Tommy and Polly seems to flit between the dynamics of a sibling rivalry; an over familiar marriage; or two bickering, but fiercely loyal, friends. The clashes, when they arrive, are intense.

'She doesn't take any prisoners,' says Steven Knight. 'And she almost knows the game better than Tommy, such as when he crosses a gangster called Billy Kimber in Series One. She preaches caution. Tommy has been lucky so far, but Polly is always warning, "You've gone too far," and Tommy always tries to push even further. He usually gets away with it, too. Some people think that Tommy's only alive because of Polly, though. She keeps him around by sometimes dragging him back from a very dangerous plan. She warns him against killing various people …'

Ada, sister to the Shelby brothers, is equally robust, marrying the communist and union agitator, Freddie Thorne (Iddo Goldberg) – a man who plays both enemy and friend to Tommy Shelby. When Ada becomes pregnant, Polly encourages the couple to leave the city. Freddie eventually refuses; shortly afterwards he draws a gun on Tommy. Later, when Ada gives birth to a son – named Karl, after Karl

Marx – Freddie is arrested by the police and beaten. The Peaky Blinders break him out of jail and he eventually sides with Tommy in a climactic battle scene with Kimber and his gang, following a turf war at the Worcester Races.

Real inspiration

'Billy Kimber was a real person,' says Knight. 'His grandson told me that, for years, they didn't talk about him in the family – they were ashamed of him. But now he's a celebrity to people. The true story seems to be that Billy Kimber got charged with murder, or assault, and went to Chicago. According to his family, he even appeared in a Charlie Chaplin film because the strong, *strong* rumour was that Charlie Chaplin was born in Birmingham on a Gypsy campsite – his mum was a circus traveller.

'I can't see any other reason why two Birmingham gangsters – Billy Kimber and one other – became his bodyguards. He must have

had a connection. When Charlie Chaplin died, he had a cabinet next to his bed. In it was a letter from somebody in Birmingham. It read something like, "I knew your mum and I know someone who was there when you were born. You were born on the Black Patch in Smethwick in Birmingham." That was the only letter he had kept.'

Other characters quickly captured the imagination during *Peaky Blinders'* opening series: Charlie Strong, the canal-yard owner and his horse-whisperer friend, Curly; Grace Burgess, the undercover police agent who later falls for Tommy – the man she's conspiring to imprison. And Sergeant Moss (Tony Pitts), a put-upon police officer, tired of working on an increasingly corrupt beat.

Throughout the richly detailed drama, Tommy Shelby, driven by the need for money and power, makes enemies easily. Manipulation is his preferred MO. And when John announces his plans to marry Lizzie Stark – a local girl known to have been a prostitute, and occasionally visited by Tommy – the Peaky Blinders' leader places her loyalty under scrutiny. Tommy asks Lizzie to sleep with him for money. When she agrees, he then announces his intention was to entrap her: Lizzie can forget marrying into the Shelby family, much to the younger brother's fury.

'I wrote that scene with the intention of using Lizzie's character once,' says Knight. 'But the actress who played her, Natasha O'Keeffe, was so good I thought, "We can't lose her – we've got to keep her." So I started to think

about what her trajectory might be. During that scene I started to plant the idea that she'd slept with Tommy quite a bit. I thought maybe she'd become attached to Tommy.'

Tommy also wars with the Lees, a feral Gypsy family living on the outskirts of Birmingham, until a peace pact is struck, facilitated by an arranged marriage between John Shelby and Esme Lee. The wedding scenes, shot by director Tom Harper, became a riotous, drunken spectacle. 'It was really cold that day and we had no time at all to do it,' says Harper. 'Sam Lee, the famous folk music artist was playing in the scene – he does a lot of Gypsy and folk music. I grew up next door to him and his album was out at the time. I remember giving him a call and seeing if he was up for doing it. He got on the train at the last minute and came in.

'Because we didn't have a lot of time to shoot the scene, it had quite an organic feel. The footage was free-flowing and handheld because we were trying to do it as quickly as we could, capturing everything as we went along. Part of the reason it had a stylistic quality was because we had to move through everything so quickly, but actually, it was really in keeping with the feeling that we'd wanted from the wedding – there was dancing, drinking and vomiting.'

The Lees and Shelbys become allies in a plot that eventually establishes the Peaky Blinders as legal, trackside bookmakers. The first step brings the Shelby's close to Billy Kimber's gang, having presented themselves as viable security for their bookies at Cheltenham racetrack. But the offer is a ruse. Tommy's real plan is to get close to Kimber, striking when he's unaware: the Lees descend upon the Worcester Races to take the Kimber turf on what Tommy calls Black Star Day, but there is a double-cross in play. Grace has discovered where the stolen guns are hidden (in a fake grave) and informs Chief Inspector Campbell, though her position is compromised: Grace has already become romantically linked to Tommy and plans to leave Birmingham, with or without him. Kimber, in the crossfire, learns of the plot to invade his territory and moves on The Garrison to attack the Peaky Blinders in the series' closing Wild West-style showdown.

Creating the look

Aside from its storytelling, what set *Peaky Blinders'* opening series apart from its contemporaries was a unique sense of design, creative twists and striking cinematography. Combining West Midlands culture with cowboy swagger – and setting the bleak themes of shell shock, communism, murder, political corruption and terrorism against a soundtrack that included Nick Cave & The Bad Seeds,

The White Stripes and The Raconteurs – the show established itself as a critical success that gathered audiences through word of mouth, rather than hype.

'What I liked about *Peaky* was that you could *smell it*,' says Helen McCrory. 'You can smell the women, the men, and the streets and the fire; the smoke and the booze. I love that smell. As a city girl, the smell of carbon monoxide, tobacco and sex is a good one. It's intoxicating.'

Within months of the show's debut on BBC2, *Peaky Blinders* was on its way to becoming a slow-burning phenomenon. Steven Knight's

reimagined spaghetti western of 'cathedrals of light', with its beautiful women and battle-scarred gangsters, had left an indelible mark on British television in more ways than one.

Post-traumatic stress disorder in postwar Birmingham

STEVEN KNIGHT: I wanted to give the very first episode of *Peaky Blinders* a theme of wildness that focused on the men coming back from the horrors of the First World War. I'd written *Hummingbird* (2013), a film with Jason Statham where the plot focused on damaged war veterans returning from Afghanistan.

I'd met a lot of Royal Marines Commandos who had come back from there with PTSD – some of their recollections later shaped the personalities and demons of Tommy and Arthur Shelby.

But I also used the trauma of war to shape Danny Whizz-Bang, a character based on Tommy Tank, the shell-shocked war veteran from my parents' childhood. In the first series, Danny believed he was still among the horrors of France, but I wanted to feed dread into all the characters. I liked the idea that Tommy, Arthur, Danny and Freddie Thorne had returned with certain memories burned into their brains. They watched them like videos in their heads, later snapping out of it and realizing they had been rocking for two or three hours, over and over.

Often, soldiers returning from the war developed a weird fear of routine, or walking home the same way twice. They worried some imaginary enemy was waiting for them. A lot of the people I spoke to with PTSD for *Hummingbird* also had a real dislike of injustice. If they were walking down the street and believed a man was being horrible to a woman, they might grab them, sensing something terrible was happening.

Danny Whizz-Bang's blackouts – where he would go into a violent frenzy, triggered by an awful war memory – were based on real accounts, too. One soldier I'd met during the making of *Hummingbird* had lost an eye in Afghanistan. He returned home and was drinking in the pub one day. The next thing he

knew, he was coming round, covered in blood. When he looked up, a policeman was staring back at him. To his horror, he realized the blood belonged to the policeman, but he couldn't remember anything about what had happened.

I placed that arc of spontaneous violence into Arthur; the ticking clock went inside Tommy and the madness into Danny Whizz-Bang. They certainly had a burning desire for revenge against the people who sent them to war – the Establishment and authority figures. And the violence was horrific.

Men came back from war traumatized. I have an uncle who was there. One time, he described a fight he'd once witnessed between two men on a bridge in Birmingham. Apparently, it was the most brutal, horrific thing he had ever seen – the two blokes were gouging each other's eyes out. They didn't have any limits; the people alongside them in war had been blown to bits by bombs and bullets and their boundaries had gone. Everybody who returned from that conflict did so with a fury inside him.

The point is that, whenever anybody experiences violence in the story, they *stay hurt* – sometimes for the whole series. There's never a situation where the injured party dusts themselves off and they're fine. It's more permanent than that. When Tommy is beaten up by Father John Hughes' men in Series Three, he goes to hospital. His eyesight is damaged and he wears glasses from then on. He also has a scar on his cheek, which is from Darby Sabini (Noah Taylor) during Series Two.

These scars are a symbol. We're reminded that just like the violence from the First World War there is a consequence to violence, one

that lasts all the way through to the Second World War. The other point is that these people, in reality, witnessed 60,000 men being blown apart in one day. A fight with a knife is less traumatic. They've seen people ripped into their component parts, so they have a numbed view on what violence is. Back then, countries were sending teenagers to their death. It's still mind-boggling what they went through.

Polly, Ada and the women behind the Peaky Blinders

STEVEN KNIGHT: I can't imagine why you wouldn't have strong female characters in a show like *Peaky Blinders*. Women ruled the roost when men came home from the pub. My mum remembered that my grandad would go out and get drunk. She'd stay up with her mum, waiting for his return. He'd come in plastered and would fall into a sofa, his hands rummaging around his pockets as he took his coat off. Often, his wages went flying around the room. It was my mum's job to get under the table to retrieve the coins because he wouldn't remember where he'd dropped them. She would then give them to her mum who would buy the food the next day.

The stories of women's lives back then were so terrible. I've not put those details into the series because some of it was too horrible, but there was a lot of domestic violence and unwanted pregnancies. One of the policeman's jobs on the beat was collecting babies. He'd

be on patrol in the morning where it wasn't uncommon to discover a box in the street with a screaming baby in it. The infant would be put into a family hospital and shipped off to Australia, where they'd sometimes be abused.

You can't underestimate the effects of alcohol in society back then. Men were drunk a lot of the time and the women had to look after the kids. They also often had to get extra money in order to keep everybody alive. It wasn't that the men didn't understand that, *they knew it was the case*. The women weren't ornaments and I wanted to reflect that here.

In *Peaky Blinders* the men are all violence and guns, but the women are the ones who control the environment. Helen, who is such a great actress, really encapsulated that idea.

HELEN McCRORY: I knew these people. These were the people that I was told about, and they were my grandparents. On my mother's side they were miners, and so researching for *Peaky Blinders* was more about remembering where my family had come from. The research I did into the women really helped me. I learned about the Birmingham police: they

would actually break up more fights started by women in Small Heath than by men. And the women would punch and fight like cats. Immediately, that told me about Polly Gray. OK, so if Polly is top of that pile ... *who the hell is Polly?* She was the most ferocious of them all.

Even though I sound like I was literally born in Buckingham Palace – well, according to my husband anyway – I actually come from a very working-class family. My mum's Welsh and my maternal grandfather was buried in the trenches (but survived) during the First World War. He was taken home, shell-shocked. He was in a wheelchair and his wife would often pick him up to bathe him, even though she was my size and he was six foot.

On the other side of the family, the Glasgow side, there were steelworkers working on the Clyde docks. These were men with big hands. I saw my grandfather, with his Glaswegian accent, sitting there smoking his pipe, a lump missing from his head that he'd have to cover up. He was one of the first Catholic foremen in a Protestant shipyard.

This whole bloody enterprise was women's business while you boys were away at war.

– Polly Gray

What I didn't know about was the greatness of Birmingham in that time and how powerful and rich it was. I love it up there, it's our turf, but it was *Peaky Blinders'* mixing of the reality of poverty and the toughness of life that appealed to me. Then on top of the story was this fable and there was a glamorization to the whole thing. Whenever agents sell an actor or actress a new part they tend to say, 'It's a bit like this.' Or, 'It's a bit derivative of that.' There was nothing to compare *Peaky Blinders* to and that was immediately exciting.

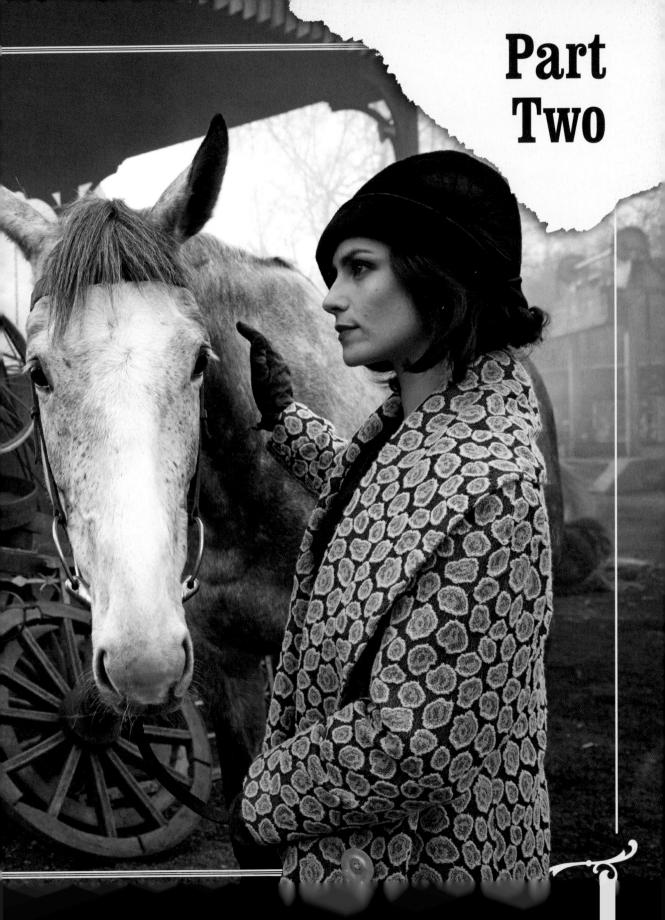

Part Two

Battlefield Birmingham

The secrets behind the sets of *Peaky Blinders.*

The Locations of *Peaky Blinders*

**NICOLE NORTHRIDGE
(PRODUCTION DESIGNER, SERIES FIVE):**

Tommy's office

It's such an iconic set and it's been in existence since Series One. Grant Montgomery, who started as production designer for Series One and Two, established the look and the feel of the show. I'd worked with Grant on a couple of productions as his supervising art director. I felt I learned a lot from him, which helped me tailor my designs into the world of *Peaky Blinders*.

Much of the research I did was looking at movies like *Once Upon a Time in America*, which I know influenced the original look of the show. I watched *The Road to Perdition*, which was a Sam Mendes movie with Tom Hanks. I got really excited as it's a visually stunning film which I felt lent itself to the look and feel of the *Peaky*-esque imagery that we've seen in the last four series. Another couple of movies I watched were *In the Mood for Love*, and *Happy Together*, which were directed by Wong Kar-wai. Even though the movies are set in the 1960s and 1990s, the texture and the colour and feel of them fitted in quite well with the *Peaky Blinders* look.

We've nicknamed Tommy's office 'The Godfather set', because I know that was a strong influence behind Grant's design for the Shelby Company office. We haven't redesigned any of this set, apart from changing some of the furniture to echo the period we are in, and we have also made up a load of new paperwork – all relevant to the company and with correct dates – to dress on desks and in folders. We've recently updated the Shelby logo, bringing it up to date for the era of Series Five. We dressed in as much other detail as we possibly could, but the actual physical structure, and the colours within the set, weren't touched. I know it's a set that Steven Knight loves.

It is a proper seat of power for the Shelby family. The desk has a real grandeur. The very dark walls keep it subdued. One of the things about *Peaky* is that it's got a graphic novel, almost abstract, feel to it. This helps focus the areas you dress as sometimes the edges of the set fall to black because of the way it's lit. A lot of thought was put into the artwork on the walls. The Shelbys are so connected to their roots. They began in the betting shop, so we had a lot of references to horses in Tommy's office, but the horses also reminded us of that infamous scene in *The Godfather*. We wanted to keep that Mafia feel going.

The Shelbys' off-track bookies

It's such a huge set. The betting shop takes up an entire studio, and it needs something like eight to ten weeks to actually set up and to refurbish. To keep them authentic and real-looking, once the plywood walls are built, they're properly plastered so that we can get that 'old wall' texture. They are then either papered or painted and aged. Once shooting, when the light catches it, the audience doesn't see them as flat walls; we see them as walls with plastering, with layers and layers of paint and paper. As you can imagine, when we break the set to pack it away for the next series, in order to get it back up, we've got a huge amount of fixing to do.

There are so many nooks and crannies in there; counting rooms and safes, offices and meeting spaces. With Finn Shelby (Harry Kirton) growing up and taking on more Shelby family responsibility, we've given him an office, which is in the betting shop. We put up racing boards with all the betting numbers on them, and we had a small counting table. It's a small flavour of what the betting shop is: that's Finn's domain.

The Garrison Tavern

For me, this was always going to be a huge undertaking. At the beginning of Series Two it is blown up and rebuilt as a Las Vegas-style drinking hall. For Series Five, when we first see it, we wanted the audience to recognize it as The Garrison Tavern, at first glance. We kept the original footprint of it, but we brought it back to a working-men's pub vibe. Story-wise, it's been seven years since we last saw it. The Shelbys have established themselves, they have money; their gauche display of new wealth is over with. We brought the pub back to the roots of Garrison Lane, which was a heavily industrialized, smoky, coal-fuelled area.

We had to make the pub all worn and scuffed. We still wanted it to be warm, inviting

and functional. It's a working man's pub and quite basic. It's almost like a western saloon, which is what it originally was in Series One.

We also tried to move it on, with a nod to the art deco look of the period. I had a lot of conversations with Anthony Byrne, our director (Series Five) about it. We are both from Ireland, which isn't short of a pub or two, and we chatted about the Dublin pubs we'd been in and loved. One of them was The Stag's Head and another was Kehoe's. We really wanted to bring in the feel of both, especially The Stag's Head, which has these fantastic stained-glass windows.

As for the other props in the pub … it took weeks to design the logos for the bottles. We went through so many variations of the Shelby Gin label before we cracked it: the logo is a white horse, and that was symbolic of hope, which was found at the bottom of a bottle of gin. We also put that design into The Garrison's etched glass mirror behind the bar, which we then aged and tarnished to try to make it look like it had been there for years. We also used many paint swatches for the walls, and a lot of lighting tests. I think we repainted the walls three or four times in different colours before we settled on the red. We felt that was quite a good colour for the show because the walls looked like they had been bathed in blood, a reference to the Shelbys' past and their rise to power.

Tommy's mansion

This was filmed in Arley Hall, a forty-minute drive south of Manchester, and it worked perfectly. The building was perfect for Tommy – it's such a cold, austere-looking building, which fits quite well with his character. In Series Three we saw more of the property, and Arley Hall was used for the exterior and for the interior downstairs. Another two big houses were used for the bedrooms and for downstairs kitchen areas. We see a lot more of Tommy's family life, but that was an amalgamation of three different big houses.

Arley Hall is open to the public and it's got a lot of light colours inside, which don't work for *Peaky Blinders*. The show's all about dark, heavy colours; we use a very dark, quite sexy colour palette. We painted the entire house. The owners have a huge number of family portraits themselves, which they own the copyright to, so we keep as many generic paintings as we can in order to fill the wall space. Obviously, some of them aren't applicable, so we have to go to 'hire houses' where we have copyright clearance, and pick relevant paintings and then we dress the entire house.

The house also hosts various functions – it's really in demand. I remember being horrified that we would only have two and a half, maybe three days at the most to dress it. In that time, we would have to strip their entire house out and turn it into a *Peaky Blinders* set. That was quite a mission.

We recently had to get three big portraits for the Shelby Company boardroom. We used an incredible artist called Desmond Mac Mahon and he painted Tommy, John and Arthur. The director and supervising art director agreed on what photos should be sent off to him – luckily there were three really good publicity shots from the last series, which worked a treat.

Desmond was then briefed on the style we wanted them in and he went to the National Portrait Gallery and spent days gathering references on Edwardian styles. He painted several oil sketches for us and sent them over. You should have seen these so-called fast sketches: they were incredible! What he produced for us was just staggering. Once the series has finished filming, all the paintings are crated up and placed in storage.

Charlie Strong's canal yard

This is located in the Black Country Living Museum in Dudley, which is open to the public and is a working canal. We only get vehicle access for all our dressing trucks before ten o'clock in the morning. Dressing it can resemble a military operation. We have to have very precise dressing timetable and dressing plans for all these large-scale set dresses. What the fans don't realize is there are so many more roads surrounding it, which makes it quite a difficult location to shoot. They've added in street lighting to the dual carriageways that surround the Living Museum, which make it very difficult to shoot at night. It looks incredible on camera though.

The tools and equipment there come from a fantastic prop house near Manchester, but the barges are there already. We design our own signage to go on each one and we have to hide some of the modern upgrades that have been made by the owners. Some of the boats are over a hundred years old, so we have to be really careful with what we do with them, and how we use them. They're items that need to be treated with a lot of respect.

The Lees' Gypsy camp

Peaky Blinders is one of the few shows I've worked on where we've had such a positive response from anybody we've asked for help when getting furniture or artwork. People love the show; it really helps that it's got such kudos and such a good reputation. But it is a hard slog as well because so much research goes into every single set and every single location. For example, we have a lot of Gypsy imagery in the show and it's vital to capture that raw Gypsy feel without making it look too romantic. The Gypsies in the late 1920s carried more of a Romany look.

We were really lucky because the company that supplied our horses, The Devil's Horsemen, own a number of period Gypsy caravans. The caravans back then were incredibly decorated. That look was a part of the culture. They also used to build tents and camps, almost like bivouacs, and we produced a lot of those, too. They were basically timber-framed, with tarpaulin and fabric covers. We then set up outside living areas like campfires, cooking areas, food prep areas and laundry stations.

I've done a huge amount of research on colonial days in India for (TV drama) *Indian Summers*, and what the British used to do there was live outside because it was so hot. Any of the furniture that was indoors was taken outside. It wasn't that uncommon to see a family sitting at a massive dining table, with all the dining chairs around it, enjoying a meal together in the open air. That feel was applicable to the Gypsies in the 1920s, too. They lived outdoors and so, for the campsite scenes, we set everything up outside.

Each person's home was broken down into areas: there was a living area, a cooking area and a washing area – all the basics for the camp. Then we put frills on it. The Gypsies in *Peaky Blinders* lived off the land and hunted a lot, so we dressed prop-made rabbits and pheasants. There was also plenty of livestock in place: we had dogs wandering around; the horses were tied up. I tried to put animals in wherever I could because it was a part of their everyday life at the time.

The Cars of *Peaky Blinders*

We use a vehicle supply company that specializes in period vehicles, but they don't necessarily have a stock of cars. What they have is a list of vintage vehicles they can call upon; they're usually owned by non-filming people. We have to keep the show in period, so we try to bring in what would have been the latest models of the time.

Frequently, we're borrowing cars from people who've never worked with a TV crew before. During filming, the owner often comes with the car and we'll always tell them which character is going to own their vehicle and what we need to do with the car because you've got to be so upfront with them as to what needs to happen to it. Like if we blow a car up …

When we do that, we go through photos of about three different types of vehicle for that period, which could double for the one we've hired. We then go to an auction and buy a clapped-out version, or to a dealer to pick up an old chassis. We'll then build a new version of that car. We'll have the proper, running, vintage model and the newly built one, which we'll hand over to special effects. They'll strip out any of the remaining fuel, clean it all up and let down the air in the tyres. If you're planning an explosion, or setting a car on fire, there are huge health and safety issues that go with it.

We'll have the actor drive up in their pristine vintage car, before cutting and swapping the vehicle out for our pre-prepped one, which is sprayed the same colour and has the same shape as the action one – it's always matching to a tee. Then special effects will blow it up and set it on fire.

The Queen

Helen McCrory on Polly Gray

The Shelbys are a family of criminals, all of them changed by a war.

When the men of *Peaky Blinders* were fighting for their country in the First World War, Polly Gray was running the Shelby family business of dealing in illegal off-track betting. And she's running it well. So when Tommy, Arthur and John return to Small Heath, she's reluctant to hand over the power. Polly doesn't really step away; her attitude is that two of them are running the show – herself and Tommy. And I think she becomes hardened as a result because women who had to run their own business when men were away at war often felt brutalized.

But everyone is brutalized in *Peaky Blinders*. Tommy and Arthur are brutalized by the war. Polly is brutalized by her life as well, especially when she loses her children to the nuns, which happens before we meet her in the story. By running a company alone, a company that's then taken off her, she constantly has to adjust to changes, even successes, and that can be equally difficult for her. When Polly gets her fancy house in Series Two, she's not jumping for joy. When she has a birthday party, she's not really celebrating either.

Polly is loving. She's loyal. She's witty. I love her attitude of calling a spade a shovel. She's good at her job and she's competent. You would want Polly on your side if ever you were in trouble. If you were stuck in a jail, in some backwater town, Polly would be the person to spring you free. She's streetwise because she is of the street and I think that's why a lot of people relate to her. Polly is what a lot of viewers would like to be when she takes bad news, externally at least. She doesn't crumble on the outside, but we see her crumble as an audience. We see her shut the door, her hand trembling as she starts to cry, but she doesn't do it in front of the other characters. Only the audience sees her pain.

Wallowing in self-pity isn't an option for Polly. She doesn't go around wailing, 'Oh, poor me! The nuns took my kids …' Or, 'Oh poor me, it's so hard to adjust …' That toughness in a person is very attractive to me. But most of all, Polly loves life and, God knows, she understands how to have a good time. She's naughty, naughty, *naughty*.

I also wanted to create that idea of danger, of Polly finding her sexuality dangerous. Polly wouldn't bring you breakfast in bed with a flower on a tray, but she'd give you a bloody good hangover. She's no prude. But she's moral. She's moral about the things she feels she needs to be moral about: love and loyalty, friendship and family.

I don't see her flaws. I don't when I'm playing a character. I'll probably be able to tell you about Polly's negative traits when

Men don't have the strategic intelligence to conduct a war between families. Men are less good at keeping secrets out of their lies.

Polly Gray

the story comes to an end. But that's a thing that one does as an actor: you never judge your character. Instead you make them marvellous. I always have to empathize with my role because if I didn't empathize with someone like Polly during her moments, I'd cheat everybody watching, especially those that have been through an identical moment; the people who know what it's like to have their kids taken away from them.

I remember somebody telling me that when you play a character, there's a triangle of ghosts behind you. They're all the people who have been in that same situation as the one you're playing, but no one has ever listened to their story before. When I say the lines, I say them for those people, and they're heard. I think of that a lot when I play Polly because I haven't heard her voice before. Everyone has tough times in life. That's what people relate to in *Peaky Blinders*. The characters aren't pretending that life isn't tough. The men are hardened by war. The women go through really horrible times, but they hold their chins up and get on with it. I admire them for that.

Polly's blind spot is undeniable, however. *It's Michael.*

Watching her two children, Michael and Anna, being taken away from her was devastating for Polly, and to play it I walked with a sense of sadness. That grief is noticeable in people who have lost their kids, even if it's years or decades after the event. You can tell. Grief changes the face, the body and the soul. And for Polly, losing both of her kids was catastrophic and she thought they were gone for ever, but that happened to so many women of that generation. When it came to researching the horror of those events, I didn't have to do too much. I only had to think of it and emotionally I was there.

What must a tragedy like that do to a person? What does it do to your dreams? It's no surprise that Polly has this third eye element about her, because she's haunted by that moment. There's also the big question mark that hangs over people that have lost their children – kids that have gone missing, or run away from home. The parents often talk about this thing of *not*

having closure. Of *not knowing where the child is.* We've read so many awful stories in the papers, such as Madeleine McCann, or the poor footballer, Emiliano Sala, who was in a plane that crashed over the English Channel – there were several days where nobody knew where his body was. The family of the missing can never rest until their child is found, until the intensity of their baby is discovered again.

That emotional pain gives the audience empathy for characters like Polly because they know her heart has been shattered into a thousand pieces. Though often the most empathetic, kindest and strongest people are those who have suffered the most.

After the initial shock of Michael's return in Series Two, Polly is filled with a great pride. It gives her a new sense of aspiration and she wants her son to do well. Interestingly she tries to change

herself in Series Three. She cuts off her hair and runs away with artists. She takes an interest in society. This is all for Michael. I don't think Polly would give a flying shit about that normally, but now that her son is back she has to be respectable. Basically she wants to save her son from the pain she experienced herself, which is what every parent wants. She warns the others, 'Michael mustn't touch a gun … Michael must be kept like this.' All of which brought in great opportunities for comedy. To see Polly suddenly minding her Ps and Qs is lovely. We don't want to be serious about these characters all the time. It's nice to laugh at them every now and then, to say, 'Oh, bless.'

But when Michael joins up with his true family, he's drawn to the darker side of the Shelbys and I've brought him to that life. He was living in a lovely place with little apple trees in the garden, where he could play football. Then I introduce him to a mob of gun-slinging, coke-snorting maniacs – this is my family! So there is a dichotomy, where Polly wants him close, but she's worried for Michael as he becomes something very different. He later begins to threaten Tommy's power in his role as part of the new generation of the Shelby business. He says to the old school, 'Your way is shit.' But that's the way of the world. And that's what's fantastic about Steve Knight's writing. He's taking a family over different dynasties, showing how they're going to fight, and where the tensions are within their lives and relationships.

I was offered the role of Polly through my agent. It was sent through as the latest thing the BBC were making that week. I was working at the National Theatre in London, opening a show with Rory Kinnear and Julie Walters called *The Last of the Haussmans* that Stephen Beresford (*Pride, Tolkien*) had written.

The *Peaky Blinders* script was sent to me and I was fascinated. I hadn't read anything like it before. It was written like a fable, like an old-fashioned odyssey of a man, in a background that I'd never heard about before. I'd never read about working-class Birmingham, and what was going on in Britain and society at that time. We'd seen it from 'upstairs', but here was 'downstairs' and Birmingham wasn't just downstairs, it was the engine room for the whole country. I realized how powerful Birmingham was at the time, how rich it was; how every street had those furnaces in them.

It was interesting because when I first looked at it, and my character, I was very confused because I didn't seem to have a mangle at any point. There weren't any scenes where I was doing the washing, or anything else that women would have been doing at that time. Steve Knight said to me, 'Watch the old westerns. Watch all of them.' I thought, 'Why does he want me to do that?' But I did and I realized that *Peaky Blinders* was an epic. It was a man against the world in Britain.

The Americans were so good at turning their working-class men into heroes on screen. So, even though Clint Eastwood was going around shooting everybody he encountered in the Wild West, while chewing a cigar, his character was still heroic. In Britain, normally, when we tell the stories of the working class and the men within it, they're victims. The idea has always been: 'Isn't it awful what happened to those men? Let's show the brutality of it all …' They threw the kitchen sink at that idea.

We'd long had that movement in our theatre and our literature: the stories of angry young men. It was shown in *Kes* and in Ken Loach's other films and many other tales. We became known for that in Britain and we did it very well. But *Peaky Blinders* was something very different. It was almost American in that way. Steve Knight wanted heroes, big characters witnessed through a child's eyes. The era was glamorized; not for a moment was *Peaky Blinders* reality. That was the fun of it; the glamour, and the fact it was about people's relatives.

Before beginning work on *Peaky Blinders*, I talked to Julie Walters while on *The Last of the Haussmans*, who of course is a Brummie. I said, 'I need an old Birmingham accent.' Julie kindly recorded two scenes from the first series, that shall remain nameless, with an old Birmingham accent. I later filmed them both on the same day and the crew came back the following morning and said, 'You can't speak like that, mate. We'll need subtitles. Nobody understands what the hell you're saying, even the other actors don't know if you've finished a sentence or not …'

So for the next scene, I went Yorkshire. Then on the next scene they said, 'No, we'll do old-fashioned Birmingham for the whole family …' Director Otto Bathurst was still getting himself together on that. He's very calm. He brought a calmness and precision to the set. Otto knows his stuff, so he had an immediate respect from everybody. I loved working with him.

Polly is the only person that Tommy sees as an equal, and vice versa. I can't speak for Cillian but I remember the first scene I did with him. I'm not sure what the hell we were talking about but we were sitting in the kitchen of the old house in Garrison Lane. I think we lit cigarettes and smoked. We talked and fought; I don't think either of us moved, apart from to inhale and exhale. Immediately I felt that was their relationship. *Polly and Tommy were the planners*. These were the plotters and the brains. It was the female side of the brain and the male side of the brain in the Peaky Blinders organization.

Despite their confrontations, Polly is fiercely protective of Tommy. They're almost like a married couple, but without the sex. There's no physical contact between them – *ever*. Tommy once put his arm around Polly when she has a surprise birthday party and both of us burst out laughing afterwards. He did it in the main take so we had to repeat it, and I remember thinking, 'What are you doing? Get off!' Cillian looked at me and said, 'That was so weird, I'm never going to touch you again.' But there's a tension between them all the time. *What are you thinking? Are you thinking what I think you're thinking?* They shouldn't be so relaxed with each other that one's putting an arm around the other.

Polly and Tommy know each other better than anyone else. They're completely different people; they're not similar in any way, but they totally respect each other. Even when Polly's telling

Men and their cocks never cease to amaze me.

Polly Gray

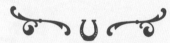

My senior position within the Shelby Company means I don't often have to ask permission from anyone to do anything.

Polly Gray

Tommy he's been a 'fucking idiot'. Or pushing him to find out his latest scheme and Tommy won't tell her because he knows she'll disapprove, so he sneaks off to a corner. Then Polly finds out anyway and comes in, all guns blazing. But no one speaks to Tommy like Polly does. And nobody is asked for an opinion like Polly is.

It's not that Polly distrusts men. Polly just distrusts. She'd be suspicious about any contract that was put in front of her, reading all the small print before committing to a signature. She does that with people as well. *Polly counts her change.* She's wary. Polly has had so many horrendous things happen to her – her husband died and then the kids were taken away – so that wasn't a great start on the relationship front for her. Then she had to give herself to Major Chester Campbell to ensure Michael's release from prison in Series Two. But she's later as traumatized when Tommy gives her the nod to kill her attacker, even though that's what she wanted to do.

I don't think in that moment Polly had ever killed anyone before. She's not one of those people.

When it comes to her love interests, Polly loves men. She distrusts herself, and I think that's the whole point. She's not a gossip; there's nothing petty about Polly. She would never sit there and go, *'Oh, men.* I just don't trust them.' But she is hurt, especially by the artist Ruben Oliver (Alexander Siddig) in Series Three. He lets her down. But much of her pain in that breakdown is due to embarrassment. Polly tries to be someone that she isn't, which is more embarrassing than when a relationship doesn't work out. That adventure was supposed to usher in the 'New Polly', one who was going to be accepted as part of society. The whole thing was shaming.

By Series Four, her life changes when she meets Aberama Gold (Aiden Gillen): the King of the Gypsies and me, the Queen, together. That was fun. I love working with Aiden. We've played lovers before and he's a very gentle, shy man, who's very nice. I enjoyed that relationship because it seemed wild and free. I like it because they're both tough, but they become very vulnerable with each other; it's very sweet. We definitely have some wild times coming.

Polly will continue to be battered by life because she lives it so fully. Anyone who lives that fully, and takes risks in that way, will be battered. But that's all right. Better that than never leaving Garrison Lane. I hope that Steve will leave her happy though, because I think, essentially, Polly *is* happy. She's one of the happiest characters in *Peaky Blinders* because Tommy is always worried about Grace and the company, and poor Arthur has a wife who doesn't always understand him, or his problems. But Polly is footloose and fancy-free. She tells everybody where to go, where to get off, and she has some pretty rock 'n' roll times along the way.

Good for her. Long may she reign.

Just Smoke and Trouble

The Shelby Company Limited expands into London: cut-throat murder, 'Tokyo'-fuelled rampages and political assassinations ensue.

An Insider's Look at Series Two

'Tommy Shelby has decided to eat the world,' says Series Two director Colm McCarthy, who previously worked on *Sherlock*, *Doctor Who* and *Ripper Street*. 'When we first meet him in the story, he has been forced to come out of his box, to lead the gang. In the next instalment he decides to push them as far as he can.'

This ambition is both violent and thrilling. Having decided to expand his business empire into London, the Peaky Blinders become embroiled in a turf war with the Italian mobster, Darby Sabini, a criminal renowned for ruling the gambling trade at a number of high-profile racetracks. Tommy decides to rattle the Sabini gang on their home turf, first by attacking and then, later, violently taking over ownership of their showpiece establishment, The Eden Club – an opulent den of London hedonism where drug-taking and sexual experimentation are out in the open.

As Steven Knight has said, the first series was about opium and the second was about cocaine – not in the drugs themselves, but the energy of the shows. That's represented in the narcotics the gang get involved in, but it's actually about the emotions within the story. So, cocaine is about excess of energy and going to the limits, whereas the opium of Series One is cocooning and softening, like being in a hot bath with sound reverberating around. Cocaine is about being edgy and being awake for too long; it's about being paranoid and over confident. That's all in there in the second series with Tommy Shelby's excesses, as he flies too close to the sun.

> ## Sir, with the greatest respect, Thomas Shelby is a murdering, cut-throat, mongrel gangster.
>
> — Major Chester Campbell

The repercussive blows land quickly. Tommy is beaten in a savage revenge attack by Sabini's gang before the assault is halted by Major Chester Campbell. It's revealed that he was able to survive the shooting by his former associate, Grace Burgess, at the end of Series One, though his wounds now force him to walk with a cane. Meanwhile, Ada Thorne, who moves house in London following the death of her husband Freddie Thorne to pestilence, is saved from the hands of Sabini's men by members of the Peaky Blinders instructed to watch her home.

In order to survive his feud with Sabini, Tommy joins forces with Alfie Solomons, a Jewish gangster from Camden, London, who is also warring with the Sabini gang. Played by Tom Hardy (*Legend*, *Dunkirk*), the character walks a fine line between ally and duplicitous enemy, threatening to switch sides when the mood takes him.

'My method of directing Tom was like Mowgli's method of managing Shere Khan,' says McCarthy. 'I felt like I had a hold of his tail and I tried to steer him. Tom wanted to create and co-author the character. When I first spoke to him on the phone, he was speaking a lot about (Alfie's character) as being a "Big bear, happy bear, angry bear…" And I was like, "So you want a beard?" Tom is a force of nature; he's unstoppable. He would absolutely attack the text and he was there because he loves Steve's writing and he loves Cillian.

'But of all the characters on the page – and Steve writes them all brilliantly – I thought, "Hmm, is Alfie going to be interesting enough?" Then as soon as Tom got hold of him he made sure that everything he did was interesting. That's what he does. Even this thing of picking his skin from his beard, it was so gross, but it was so engrossing and interesting as well. ("Tom loved his psoriasis, and he always wanted more," says hair and make-up designer, Loz Schiavo, of Hardy's complexion. "In his last series we gave him quite a lot.") Cillian and Tom get on really well and were doing *Big Lebowski* scenes with each other between takes.'

Following a truce between Darby Sabini and Alfie Solomons, the Peaky Blinders find themselves betrayed and outnumbered, but this union is short-lived. Darby Sabini double-crosses the Camden gangster, who soon sides with Tommy once more. Ownership of The Eden Club is reclaimed by Sabini, but power swings back again to the Peaky Blinders at the end of Series Two when they defeat Sabini's men at the Epsom Derby, burning their licences and taking control of the track for their own bookmaking affairs.

The power of yearning

Tommy has other troubles, however. Bruised by Grace Burgess's betrayal in Series One, he sleeps with the horse trainer May Carleton, a rich widow initially employed to prepare his newly purchased horse for racing. Tommy chooses a somewhat masochistic name for the animal: *Grace's Secret*. 'The theme of Series Two is yearning,' says McCarthy. 'A lot of people are yearning in the story. It was a word that was swirling around my brain a lot as we were making it. There's a desire for more than is available, or possible – it's the unquenchable thirst that exists in a lot of the characters. They're defined by what they can't have and Tommy's appetite is expanding.'

But Tommy's desire to become a part of the Establishment and to move into more legitimate business practices is a hurdle that will, at times, seem insurmountable. 'I wanted to explore, in a tangible way, the class system,' says Steven Knight. 'Tommy meets May and she's obviously from a rich background. He has money, but there's a metaphor in that they're both bidding for the same horse during an auction: financially they're the same, but they're both from a different class. She lost her officer husband in the war.

'In the twenties, the class barriers were breaking down a bit. In D. H. Lawrence and Thomas Hardy novels the characters aspire to move up in class. If you look at the *Daily Mail* and other newspapers at the time, there was a sense of horror that upper-class women were being courted by working-class men. They were also scared by the Chinese, who they called "The Yellow Peril". Those papers

had noticed that society parties were in an age of hedonism with cocaine and booze. A lot of parties would invite gangsters – and it was the same in America – to titillate the guests.

'At rich gatherings you'd have the local bootlegger, or cocaine dealer, and he'd often be from the working class. People were horrified that women could be attracted to these men. I wanted to explore that class thing, without being too on the nose. The link between Tommy and May in the story is the horse, and with Tommy all bets are off when horses are involved. That's all he loves. At one point he even says, "I am a horse". So that connection between two very different people from two very different backgrounds was a way of obliquely looking at class systems and what was going on back then.'

> **When I drove into Small Heath I thought I was going to get murdered. Then I mentioned your name. It was like being escorted to see a king.**
>
> **– May Carleton to Tommy Shelby**

Tommy has other entanglements, however. When Grace returns from America – where she has married a wealthy banker – to see a fertility doctor in London, they endure an initially tense meeting before the ice thaws considerably: Tommy takes Grace to a party where she is introduced to Charlie Chaplin. After a brief affair, she falls pregnant with Tommy's baby.

'The scenes with Grace and Tommy, and the wrestling between their relationship and the one with Tommy and May was really interesting,' says McCarthy. 'The crew and cast were rooting for different individuals. Some were on Team May, others on Team Grace, and it was very interesting how that story unfolded. It was partly a conversation about female characters and it was partly about the relationship people had with the characters. The actors all had a really good time doing it.

'Charlotte and Annabelle are very different actors. They have a different methodology. Charlotte is very cerebral and talks through things a lot; Annabelle is instinctive. Neither way is right or wrong – they're both lovely and smart – but they're very different to each other. I wanted people to be conflicted by Tommy's choices throughout. Sometimes there can be a version of that kind of story where we lose an understanding for a character's (in this case, Tommy's) situation. We had to present both May and Grace as being interesting to Tommy, but it was important that they were both active in his story. Neither of them was supposed to look like a victim, and that was really important. I didn't want that to happen.'

There are familial issues to deal with, too. Arthur descends into madness. He kills a

young man during a bloodlust assault when a boxing match gets out of hand. Later, Arthur is introduced to 'Tokyo', or cocaine; the drug quickly heightening his mania and anarchic energy until he becomes hooked. Tommy has to confront him, hauling Arthur back from the brink by telling him that if he doesn't shape up he'll strip him of The Eden Club management role and hand the responsibility to John.

'Paul just makes himself feel that stuff for real,' says McCarthy. 'And it made my hair stand up on end. I remember in the scene when he and Tommy confront each other, being concerned that somebody was going to get hurt. On the one hand, I wanted everybody to feel all right. But on the other it was exciting because it meant something real was going on.

'I remember talking to him before filming started and him saying, "I love playing this guy." I wound up having a really enjoyable collaboration with Paul. He's not like anybody else I've ever met, he's incredibly entertaining and he can be really funny.

'We were shooting the scene when Tommy leaves the party (when The Garrison Tavern reopens after being blown up at the opening to Series Two). He goes to the back of the pub and takes out a letter from Grace and burns it. In the background, the party is still going on and Arthur was involved. We were shooting with Cillian and I said, "I think it really helps if the party feels like it's in full swing." I said that to Paul and he absolutely went for it. Afterwards, the prop person came up to me, looking really disturbed and said:

'Yeah, he's just gone through forty-eight bottles of champagne.'

'How do you mean?'

'Well, we had lots of sugar-glass bottles of champagne and he's smashed them all.'

'With Paul, it's never about any kind of ego. There's a real purity to him and his desire to immerse himself completely in the character. But I think Arthur is a very tough character to be inside.'

Elsewhere, Tommy becomes enmeshed in a complex political web and is coerced into the assassination of a blacksmith by the pro-Treaty Irish Republican group. Major Campbell, aware of this murder, blackmails Tommy into assassinating Field Marshal Henry Russell (James Richard Marshall); the hit has been ordered by Winston Churchill (Richard McCabe) on behalf of the Crown. Campbell uses his powerful influence to cajole Tommy into action, threatening his family and business interests.

With time running out, a bloody ending to a most violent endeavour looks inescapable for Tommy Shelby.

Throughout Series Two, Polly Gray's 'yearning' focuses on her missing children. She mourns for the son and daughter placed into care when her life crumbled. Haunted by their absence, she visits a Gypsy medium to learn of their whereabouts and is told her daughter is dead. This truth is confirmed by Tommy when he uncovers paperwork from the parish responsible for their upbringing. Her surviving son, Michael, is later located and turns out to be a character very much in the same mould as the Peaky Blinders' villainous totem. When Tommy and Michael meet, the young man talks of his desire to blow up the wishing well positioned in his home village. Before that, he startles Polly by introducing himself on her front door as she staggers home from a one-night stand.

'Polly comes back from a party looking like Janis Joplin,' says Helen McCrory. 'Michael is standing there. He says, "Is this the house of Polly Gray?" In the script she realizes who it is, but in the original take – and this actually happened for real and definitely was *not* scripted – I turned around and vomited on the street with the shock. It was really weird. It was so primal. Everybody on the crew shouted, "Arrrrgh! *Cut!*" But that's what the shock would be like in your body if your son returned out of the blue, standing there, and with all the confusion. I think the crew were so horrified at my acting choice, the scene was cut.

> # I imagine being shot by a woman hurts the same as being shot by a man. Just a bit more shameful. You know, Mr Campbell, when I got shot, they gave me a medal. No medal for you, I bet.
>
> **– Tommy Shelby**

'It was natural, though. *Peaky Blinders* looks great. Not because we have any money, let me assure you – *Peaky Blinders* is not expensive, but it *looks* expensive because of people's artistry. We film so quickly, which means we become familiar with the scenes beforehand, knowing the lines inside out and backwards. I imagined where Polly has been in the build up to that moment; I had the costume on and threw myself into it to then see what came up.

'It's only at that moment that I see everybody's work. I see how Finn is going to play Michael and how the director is going to see it. I see the set, whether there are other people on the streets. I'm seeing all that for the first time. Then, having done that preparation, you shut off all those other people's work at your peril, because that's all helping the scene. I have to be very alert, but I also have to leave myself alone to see what takes place when the filming starts.

'And what happens when I meet Michael for the first time? *I chuck up in the street.*'

An eye for an eye

But, like Tommy's yearning for expansion and Arthur's attempts to free himself from mental anguish, Polly's fantasy of reconnecting with her son is confronted by some uncomfortable realities. Michael's interest in the darker aspects of the Peaky Blinders' business draws him closer to risk and violence. He watches as the gang are fired upon during a horse auction and Arthur brutally assaults one of their attackers. When Michael later goes drinking with Isiah

(Jordan Bolger) – son of Jeremiah Jesus – at The Marquis of Lorne, they are racially abused and become caught up in a bar fight. The pub is later razed to the ground in an act of retribution.

This act sees Michael imprisoned by Major Campbell, but the punishment is used as leverage: if the newest member of the Peaky Blinders (Michael is eventually given the role of company accountant) is to be set free, then Tommy has to carry out his assassination of Field Marshal Henry Russell. Polly forces the issue, offering herself to Campbell in his office in order to secure her son's release, during a horrific sexual assault.

'Everybody is always sympathetic to the actor playing the victim in those scenes,' says Colm McCarthy. 'But it's a really hard thing to do if you're a person like Sam Neill (Major Campbell), who's a lovely guy and the least aggressive person you could imagine. For him to play that scene was a *very* difficult place for an actor to go to. Sometimes on set that can be awkward for someone who's playing a horrible character when they're not a horrible person themselves. They're often quite sensitive people, but they're making themselves very raw by playing out a difficult scene.

'Both Polly and Sam were really good with each other. They both made it OK for each other and were laughing a lot in between takes and having a good time. It was their way of making it safe. Actors need a safe place where they don't feel rushed, harassed or hassled,

but feel like they've got room to do the work they need to do. They both made each other comfortable enough to go somewhere as dark as that scene had to go.'

Michael is released shortly afterwards. When Polly meets him at the prison gates, he makes her aware of his shame, the prison guards having revealed the lengths to which his mother was prepared to go to in order to ensure his speedy pardon. But, for Polly, the fallout from Campbell's assault has left both psychological and physical scars; she gets drunk and attempts to wash away her emotional tumult.

'That scene was Helen's idea,' says McCarthy. 'A lot of actors have ideas and they're often quite selfish; they're designed to make them look good. Helen's ideas were really about drilling into what the material was trying to do; they were thoughts about staging. Originally, she was scripted to return home drunk, but Helen made the suggestion that Polly might be already home when we next see her, drinking in the bath, trying to wash herself clean. That was such a good instinct and it was a very powerful moment.

'I remember that Helen had a folder, like a secondary school kid's folder, with ideas stuck to her script and notes on the character. But at the same time, she's never at all pushy. She doesn't attempt to take over. She's just incredibly generous with her ideas and when she pitched up on set, she'd written a poem about her time on the second series of *Peaky Blinders* and she read it out to the crew. It wasn't a big deal, but she mentioned everybody: the runners, the assistant make-up people, everyone. Herself and Cillian are very generous with the people they work with, both creatively and on a human level.'

With the Crown's assassination plot in motion, Tommy kills Field Marshal Henry Russell at the Epsom Derby. In the chaotic aftermath, Tommy is bundled into the back of a truck by soldiers of the Ulster Volunteer Force, associates of Major Campbell known as the Red Right Hand. He is to be executed and dumped in a hastily dug grave.

Polly is later able to exact her revenge on Major Campbell and shoots him dead as he makes a phone call to Winston Churchill, explaining that the instructions to have Field Marshal Henry Russell executed have been carried out and that Tommy Shelby has also been sent to his death, having been kidnapped by the Red Right Hand. 'But I don't think in that moment that Polly has ever killed anyone before,' says McCrory. 'I don't feel like she's one of *those* people.'

Don't fuck with the Peaky Blinders.

— Polly Gray

Luckily for Tommy, he is soon given a reprieve. Kneeling over a shallow grave, and with an executioner's revolver at his head, two shots ring out – one for the gunman, the other for his accomplice. The third kidnapper, it turns out, is working as a double agent.

'At some point in the near future, Mr Churchill will want to speak to you in person, Mr Shelby,' explains the mysterious rescuer. 'He has a job for you.'

Having escaped execution and with the Shelby family's enterprises set to expand ever larger, Tommy then informs Michael of his plan to get married.

'One of the things that's brilliant about Tommy as a character and Cillian as an actor is that we're fascinated by him, but we're also

trying to figure out what's going on in his head,' says McCarthy. 'That's a huge part of the compulsion to watch the show. We want to figure out what Tommy's plan is and who he really loves. *What's really going on inside his heart?* Because while he can be considered a bad guy, there's a lot of debate regarding that: *is he a bad guy, or is he somebody who does bad things?*

'He's burned by a desire to hold his family together, to look after those he cares about, and do right by his community. He's always fighting somebody that's nastier than him. And yet, he's willing to do bad things, *really bad things*, while using people along the way. When he has somebody that he feels is worse than him according to his own moral code – though Tommy wouldn't call it a moral code – he will be unbelievably shitty towards them. And Steven Knight writes that so brilliantly.'

The story of Alfie Solomons

STEVEN KNIGHT: Alfie was a real person, a Jewish gangster from London, and was sometimes allied to and sometimes an enemy of Darby Sabini, another real Italian gangster. My dad told me that Little Italy in Birmingham was just down the road from where he grew up and there were a lot of Italians there. Obviously, a lot of them were in cahoots with Sabini, so the reality of that was great.

Here's an example of how sometimes nice bits of the *Peaky Blinders* story can come about accidentally. When I wrote Alfie Solomons, he had a rum distillery, but when we were looking for a location we couldn't find a real distillery. The next best space was a bakery, and when we filmed there it was quite obviously a bakery, so we made that a ruse for Alfie: *it's an illegal distillery disguised as a bakery.* It makes him look clever.

When he meets Tommy for the first time, he says, 'I make white bread, and I make brown bread.' And he puts down two glasses of rum, but that was an accident caused by a loss of location. The script didn't change. I wanted Alfie to feel unexpected as a really tough Jewish guy. I took bits and pieces from real life. The fact that he was in Camden is important because the canals are there, and that canal goes all the way to Birmingham; they're connected.

Tom and myself first worked on the film *Locke*. I loved working with him, it was great to do, and when I wrote Series Two of *Peaky Blinders*, I thought, 'I'd like Tom for the part of Alfie. Oh well, I'll give it a go.' I gave him the script and now he loves that character. He took it over and forged the role, making it his own.

The death of Freddie Thorne

SOPHIE RUNDLE: Freddie dies between Series One and Two from pestilence, and the story becomes a mosaic, where we hear of these little things happening off screen. Ada is one of those people that, when something hurts her, or she takes something to heart, she takes it very privately. I think Freddie's death will forever be painful and it comes up afterwards, but it's usually only fleeting.

For men and women, that's what they did in those days: they didn't linger on their emotions, or talk about them, or have therapy sessions where they explored the ramifications of the turbulent events affecting them. They took their pain and they locked it away, and that's a part of Ada's story. Her pain is buried deeper than any of us will ever know, but while she's locked it away, it will always be there.

It haunts Ada because Freddie is her son's father, but Freddie's death serves to make her stronger. It didn't debilitate her in the way that grief can. When Tommy loses Grace in Series Three, it drags him down.

Part
Three

Go Across the Tracks

The story behind the music of *Peaky Blinders.*

STEVEN KNIGHT: I think Cillian Murphy said it best: 'There are certain songs that are *Peaky*, and certain songs that are not.' They could be by the same artist, but there's something about the attitude, the lyricism and the sadness and the sensibility. There's a real heavy melancholy to *Peaky* songs.

**AMELIA HARTLEY
(HEAD OF MUSIC, ENDEMOL):**
Johnny Cash was an amazing musician, but he had a pretty difficult life. We can hear that in his voice, his lyrics and in what he's singing. It's the same with Tom Waits. For *Peaky Blinders* we use artists who you can tell have got a story.

What is the spirit of a *Peaky Blinders* song? I think that it's authenticity.

Normally, we're working very much in an area with songwriters, people writing from their own experiences, and then expressing that in the character (in a song). That really relates to our characters.

The songs are gothic and dark-hearted because the story has come out of the First World War and all the experiences the characters have had. Birmingham at that time was gritty, dark. The music is a reflection of the furnaces and smoke, whether that's coming out of being bombed during the war or the factories and the industry. It's a very industrial setting in the first couple of series. I think that's very much reflected in the instrumentation, which is very rocky, raw and gritty. That's where our palette has come from: it's by the troubadour, a singer-songwriter producing very complicated, authentic material.

**JAMIE GLAZEBROOK
(EXECUTIVE PRODUCER):**
I loved the fact that the music shook you out of any sense of thinking that *Peaky Blinders* was a period drama. It hopefully made everything feel more present.

HELEN McCRORY: I remember (Series One director) Otto Bathurst calling me up and saying, 'I really need music for the show, like The White Stripes …' I knew the lawyer for The White Stripes and Otto wanted me to call him. I said, 'Really, Otto? Why do you want me to call Jack White and ask for his music? What are you doing here?' I thought the soundtrack was going to be 'You Are My Sunshine', or whatever the music was in the 1920s. Or maybe some dark Scandi noir thing, but not what we ended up with.

Anyway, we showed a cut version of *Peaky Blinders* to Jack White, who said, 'Yes, they can use my stuff.'

JAMIE GLAZEBROOK: I think the music, especially (opening credits soundtrack) 'Red Right Hand' by Nick Cave & The Bad Seeds, managed to evoke an outlaw feel. We realize we're watching something that has a spaghetti western feel in there. The Wild West was always in our minds, so a sense of swagger was important to us.

The music was a brilliant thing brought by

Otto Bathurst, our first director, and as we went deeper into the series we realized there was a great opportunity for those musical voices to evoke and comment on the state of mind of our characters, particularly Tommy Shelby. That was such an interesting journey, hearing the confident swagger of Jack White, to a more emotional PJ Harvey theme in Series Two. Then, when you go into Series Three, the sense of existential crisis that Radiohead brings kept with the story.

We've used the music as a way in to the characters' heads, and that might be the secret of it working. It's never there just to give an episode an injection of energy, or to be cool. It's always about the internal monologue of the characters.

AMELIA HARTLEY: You can use commercial music for all kinds of things: you can use it to bridge a couple of shots; you can use it to reflect the emotion of what's happening; or you can use it to drive the scene on. But what we try to do is to be a mirror of what's happening in the characters' heads.

You soon get to know all the characters, and you get to understand what musical area they're in, because there's a defined palette now. We choose artists that are quite complex, and intelligent in the music they produce because it really helps us to reflect the characters and their complexity.

That's why Radiohead have worked really well, such as in the scene in which Tommy has a breakdown by the lake in Series Four, episode six. 'Pyramid Song' plays. It's as much

a reflection of his confusion and the utter, utter despair of what he's become and how conflicted he is. What he's dealing with is reflected beautifully in the music.

How do we choose the songs? Hardly anything is scripted, so you can't really choose from simply reading through the story. It's only once we've seen the scenes to see how the plot plays out and how everything's been shot that we can start working. We'll always get the scripts, so I'll know what the storylines are and where a particular series is heading; whether it's back in deepest, darkest Birmingham, like Series Four, or set in the beautiful countryside of Series Three, when Tommy had become newly affluent. That gives us a feel for the plot and mood.

This means we have a different voice for every series, because each one is moving the story of the Shelbys on. After the first series we had the cocaine years (Series Two). By Series Three, Tommy has money, so there's a different feel. We'll always have an artist to reflect that change. For example, Series One was Nick Cave & The Bad Seeds and Jack White; on Series Two it was PJ Harvey and the Arctic Monkeys. By the time we'd hit Series Three, it was David Bowie and Leonard Cohen, to reflect the story's evolution. A lot of people in the music industry are big fans of *Peaky Blinders*. We've been lucky enough to get people to say yes to being featured in the show and that's quite unusual, given the high calibre of artist we approached.

THE MUSIC SOCIET

it's an

CONCERT

featuring

David Bowi
Radiohead
Arctic Monkey
PJ Harve
Tom Wait

with

NICK CAVE & THE BAD SE

performing 'Red Right Ha

Tickets: 8/6 5/9 2/

may be obtained from the box office of the

Lazarus

78 RPM

Records are not exchanged or sent on approval

The Largest stock of records in Birmingham

David Bowie

SOUND RECORDINGS LIMITED
Small Heath, Birmingham.

PAUL ANDERSON: We could have used long, drawn-out piano music from the 1920s, period style. But it was Otto who wanted to use these new bands. At first, I was a bit unsure about it, because using rock bands against drama might have sounded a little contrived. But when I heard some of the music they had and saw the end result it really worked.

I loved it. It's flattering. And to know that David Bowie – God rest his soul – knows that I was in the show; to think that he was watching me, and getting pleasure out of my art form when I've been getting pleasure out of his art form for years … It was amazing. How incredible is that?

FINN COLE: Going into the second series as a new character was really cool, because I was aware of the music … So, I was more aware of what the final picture was going to look like, the final story. I knew the shots they were doing, why they were doing them. So,

I enjoyed walking down the street knowing there was going to be some Nick Cave or Arctic Monkeys playing in the background. I could almost play to that a little bit.

AMELIA HARTLEY: Music-wise, we definitely punch above our weight in terms of influence, and we are well known for our use of music: we've now got one of the biggest unofficial Spotify playlists around.

After each episode airs at ten o'clock, the BBC put up the playlist of commercial music, and that's been their most popular playlist, and we regularly feature in the Billboard top 10 of TV programmes which are influential in music.

HELEN McCRORY: It's such fun to do this. We went to see The Rolling Stones the other day and I said to Ronnie Wood, 'Oh man, look at you! You're a fucking Rolling Stone.' Ronnie looked at me and said, 'Yeah babe, but you're a fucking Peaky Blinder.'

AUTHORISED DEALERS — FOR — Columbia

ARABELLA

ARCTIC MONKEYS

78 RPM

SOUND RECORDINGS LIMITED
Small Heath, Birmingham.

The Story Behind the Soundtrack

'Red Right Hand', Nick Cave & The Bad Seeds: Series One

AMELIA HARTLEY: We've done so many covers of 'Red Right Hand': Arctic Monkeys have covered it, Laura Marling covered it for us. There's an Iggy Pop cover of it. PJ Harvey's covered it for us. We've done remixes, we've done stripped-back versions, it's an amazing piece of songwriting and we are so lucky to be able to have it as our title music.

The tolling bell sound that features in the track is just so reflective of the industrial backdrop of Birmingham, in terms of its sound: it's menacing, it's dark. It also has a religious undertone to it, which I quite like, because there are religious themes running as undercurrents through many of our storylines.

'Lazarus', David Bowie: Series Three

STEVEN KNIGHT: We were finishing Series Three and we were looking at music and I was saying, 'Let's aim high. Let's go for Leonard Cohen, Bob Dylan and David Bowie ...' No one knew Bowie was ill at that time, but his people came back to us and said, 'He's a big fan of the show and he'd love to have his music on it.' I couldn't believe it. We had also got a response from Leonard Cohen – so I'd got two of my heroes on board.

It was coming up to Christmas and Bowie's people said, 'We'd love you to listen to some stuff.' It was the album he released recently,

Blackstar, but at the time nobody had heard it. They wanted to see if there was any stuff we wanted to use and sent someone to my house to play it to me, because they couldn't send it in a form that was secure enough.

When they played me 'Lazarus', I couldn't believe it. I said, 'We'll take it all! If he wants to come to the set, if he's such a fan, he can ...' The representative promised to extend my offer, but on the Tuesday or Wednesday of that week I heard on the radio that he had died. I did not have a clue he was ill. Not many people did. I think a couple of years earlier in New York, Cillian had met him because David Bowie wanted to meet *him*. Cillian gave Bowie the cap he wore in Series One with the razor blades. Bowie sent him back a photo of himself wearing it; that's how we knew he was a fan.

'This Is Love', PJ Harvey: Series Three

AMELIA HARTLEY: One of my favourite scenes in the story is where Polly enters a party in Series Three. PJ Harvey's 'This Is Love'

Arthur

Thomas

is playing as she comes in. She's wearing a sensational dress, she's in control of her love life, the Shelbys are on the up and she totally owns her entrance to the party. The brilliant track adds to her movement and power. Ultimately, though, there is also something raw and compromised about this scene, as underlining it is the feeling that, as a Shelby, falling in love just might not be possible, so the music also reflects a certain sadness.

It was great to give Polly a female vocal, especially someone with such amazing vocals as PJ Harvey. Artists such as The Kills, Laura Marling and PJ Harvey are great to have in the series to add further complexity to our musical palette and help reinforce our strong female characters, as well as being just generally great tracks to soundtrack our action.

Polly looks so amazing in that scene, and she's as hard as nails, but actually underneath it all, like anyone, she clearly wants someone to love and to be loved. Polly is really putting herself out there in this moment and comes swanning in. I think this scene speaks to women, because she just looks so amazing, and she swaggers, with this amazing song behind her.

It's a really central moment in terms of everything coming together to bring forward how she feels, but there's a pathos about it, because her nascent relationship with the painter, Ruben, probably isn't going to last. She's from a family where everyone who gets near to them has an ulterior motive, or they might get scared off. In this scene, with PJ

Harvey playing, we're rooting for her but at the same time we're worried she's going to get hurt, in the most basic way.

'You And Whose Army?', Radiohead: Series Three

JAMIE GLAZEBROOK: Sometimes there are amazing, happy accidents when putting together the music for *Peaky Blinders*. I remember finding the Radiohead song from *Amnesiac* – 'You And Whose Army?' – which goes at the end of the first episode of Series Three. It's a song of two or three stages, and that just went onto a sequence that had already been cut to that shape: it was bizarre – it just landed.

AMELIA HARTLEY: It was the perfect, perfect match. The Radiohead pieces are just brilliant, and this one when the body is being buried and the Peaky Blinders all come out of the mansion before driving to Small Heath worked so well. And what Radiohead have to say is incredibly intelligent and thought-provoking and rich, and so are the storylines that we're trying to reflect, as are the characters. Nothing's one-dimensional about them at all.

78RPM

Series One

'Red Right Hand' – Nick Cave & The Bad Seeds

'Hardest Button To Button' – The White Stripes

'Blue Veins' – The Raconteurs

'Zanstra' – Nick Cave and Warren Ellis

'St James Infirmary Blues' – The White Stripes

'Abattoir Blues' – Nick Cave & The Bad Seeds

'When I Hear My Name' – The White Stripes

'Martha's Dream' – Nick Cave and Warren Ellis

'Broken Boy Soldier' – The Raconteurs

'Clap Hands' – Tom Waits

'I Fought Piranhas' – The White Stripes

'God Is In The House'
– Nick Cave & The Bad Seeds

'Little Cream Soda' – The White Stripes

'Ball And Biscuit' – The White Stripes

'Love Is Blindness' – Jack White

The Prowl' – Dan Auerbach

Series Two

'Arabella' – Arctic Monkeys

'What He Wrote' – Laura Marling

'Working For The Man' – PJ Harvey

'Catherine' – PJ Harvey

'One For The Road' – Arctic Monkeys

'C'mon Billy' – PJ Harvey

'Red Right Hand' – Arctic Monkeys

'Out Of The Black' – Royal Blood

'All And Everyone' – PJ Harvey

'Loverman' – Nick Cave & The Bad Seeds

'Pull A U' – The Kills

'Rocking Horse' – The Dead Weather

'Danny Boy' – Johnny Cash

'Gonna Make My Own Money' – Deap Vally

'I Want Some More' – Dan Auerbach

'Dance Little Liar' – Arctic Monkeys

'Fried My Little Brains' – The Kills

'River Styx' – Black Rebel Motorcycle Club

'All My Tears' – Ane Brun

Series Three

'You And Whose Army?' – Radiohead
Dangerous Animals' – Arctic Monkeys
'Breathless' – Nick Cave & The Bad Seeds
'This Is Love' – PJ Harvey
'I Might Be Wrong' – Radiohead
'Crying Lightning' – Arctic Monkeys
'DNA' – The Kills
'Used To Be My Girl'
– The Last Shadow Puppets
'Don't Sit Down 'Cause I've Moved
Your Chair' – Arctic Monkeys
'Soldier's Things' – Tom Waits
'Tupelo' – Nick Cave & The Bad Seeds
'Burn The Witch'
– Queens Of The Stone Age
'Red Right Hand' – PJ Harvey
'Bad Habits' – The Last Shadow Puppets
'Meet Ze Monsta' – PJ Harvey
'Monkey 23' – The Kills
'Baby Did A Bad Bad Thing' – Queen Kwong
'Cherry Lips' – Archie Bronson Outfit
'Lazarus' – David Bowie
'Life In A Glasshouse' – Radiohead

Series Four

'Adore' – Savages
'Red Right Hand' – Fidlar
'Alas Salvation' – Yak
'Further On Up The Road' – Johnny Cash
'Mercy Seat'
– Nick Cave & The Bad Seeds
'Lost' – TOMMYANDMARY
'The Longing' – Imelda May
'Devil Inside Me'
– Frank Carter & The Rattlesnakers
'I Wish, I Wish'
– Rachel Unthank & The Winterset
'Beat The Devil's Tattoo'
– Black Rebel Motorcycle Club
'Snake Oil' – Foals
'Heart Of A Dog' – The Kills
'Saved These Words' – Laura Marling
'Red Right Hand'
– Iggy Pop and Jarvis Cocker
'A Hard Rain's Gonna Fall' – Laura Marling
'Pyramid Song' – Radiohead

The Preacher

Benjamin Zephaniah on Jeremiah Jesus

I know Birmingham very well – I was born and raised there. And though I didn't see the city as it was portrayed in *Peaky Blinders*, I witnessed the end of the industrial age. When I was a kid, the streets were surrounded by factories. There was Canning's, which produced metal plating, and Lucas's – they made the lights for almost every car in the world. There was British Leyland and the munitions plant, Birmingham Small Arms factory, which appeared in Series One, though they originally produced guns for the war and ended up manufacturing motorbikes.

The end of that era coincided with the beginning of heavy metal music in the seventies and the city had something to do with its name. Birmingham was a place of heavy metals: they even have the Jewellery Quarter. I also remember the smog, walking out into the street and not being able to see much in front of my face because there was so much smoke and pollution belching from people's domestic chimneys, as well as the factories. Birmingham was foggy; I'd walk down the street and I'd see a shadow coming towards me in the mist, a shape, or I'd hear somebody calling my name. It was only once I'd got close enough that I could make out a person I knew.

When it came to filming *Peaky Blinders*, it didn't take a lot to imagine what it might have been like living in that era between the First World War and the Second World War because it was only a few decades prior to my childhood. I saw the hangover from that period. When we watch those scenes in *Peaky Blinders*, where the fires are burning by the factories and the smog is hanging in the streets, it's not alien to me at all. That's how I remembered it. That all changed when the Clean Air Act happened in 1956 and people had to burn a type of coal that didn't produce as much smoke.

But it was such a different time then in so many ways. In the show, Jeremiah Jesus doesn't experience racism, not the kind we would see further on in British history. According to Steve Knight, the real character, Jimmy Jesus, was followed around by kids who thought he was a novelty. They hadn't seen anyone from the Caribbean before and there wasn't the type of bigotry that later emerged, where people complained, 'They're here to take our jobs.' Instead, people wanted to hear what black people had to say. The kids from Birmingham were interested in talking to somebody from Jamaica, or Africa. I'd chat to black people who were here during the war, and after the Second World War. They often told me, 'We were novelties. When we went into a club, the girls knew that we could dance and they'd come to us.'

A long time before the Peaky Blinders gang, a black man called Olaudah Equiano came over. He was a freed slave and went to Birmingham in 1790, where he was welcomed because

> *The Lord will smite the unholy when judgement comes… and judgement is coming, my friends.*
>
> Jeremiah Jesus

there was such a strong anti-slavery movement in the city. Equiano packed out the halls whenever he spoke about slavery; apparently, at that time a lot of shackles intended for slaves were made in Birmingham, so the women refused to have sex with their husbands if they worked for the manufacturers producing the binds. Other people refused to buy sugar if they knew it came from the colonies, recognizing it had been produced through slavery.

That all changed by the time I came to live in Birmingham. I went to a school called St Matthias and it was terrible. I hated it, but it was only afterwards that I realized why. When I turned up, they automatically made me the captain of the cricket team, even though I couldn't stand the sport. I later learned they had actually started the cricket team in the first place … *because of me*. I remember Muhammad Ali was in his prime, winning fights all the time, but I hated that too because all the kids at school expected me to fight like him.

Because St Matthias was a religious school, we had prayers every morning. One day I went to the toilet and splashed the seat a little. I was only five or six years old but the teacher brought me out in front of the whole school. Can you imagine? I'm the only black kid there, apart from my twin sister, and the teacher was speaking to me in front of everybody.

'In this country, our little boys lift the toilet seat before we wee in there, don't we, boys?' she said.

The boys in the school all responded: *Yes, miss.*

She went on. 'In this country, little boys do this, and little boys do that …'

Yes, miss. Yes, miss.

It was so confusing.

Every now and then the Gypsies would come through town. I went to a Protestant school, and down the road was a Catholic school, but the Protestants didn't like the Gypsies. They said, 'They're dirty, they do this and do that.' But I loved them. They played in the dirt. They played in the bombsites. They'd make

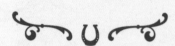

Tommy: Jeremiah, can you ask Him from me, if you can help us today?

Jeremiah: God says he don't deal with Small Heath, sir.

things and fix things, and they were *really* good at fixing things. If you had a broken bike, they'd fix it up and knock it about and put it together for you. Then, at the end of the evening, they'd sit around the campfire and read poems and sing songs. They were almost Caribbean to me.

I used to make this joke that all their girls had scars, because they'd often fight as much as the boys. I remember sitting round their campfire in the evening, my bike fixed, and a couple of them would walk me back home afterwards. I was telling Packy (Lee, who plays Johnny Dogs in *Peaky Blinders*) about this on set. I went through the stories about what they used to do, and he started singing the songs. All the memories came back!

But when *Peaky Blinders* started, some people were talking about the accents; they complained. The truth is this: the Birmingham accent has evolved. When I was young, I can remember how influenced by Irish the Birmingham accent was, because there was a big Irish community there. That was depicted in *Peaky Blinders*, because it must have been even more relevant during that era – in Series One the IRA, the original IRA, had strong support in Birmingham.

Two friends of mine were killed by the IRA in the Birmingham bombing – a terrorist attack that took place in 1974, killing twenty-one people. I was a small-time crook then; I was even in a gang that used to call ourselves the Rastafarian Peaky Blinders. A few of us were on bail, already in trouble with the law, when two mates, Paul and Neil, went missing. The police hounded us – they wanted to know where they were and why they hadn't checked in on bail – until one day, they knocked on our door with a priest. We knew it was serious because usually they wanted to know if we had any hidden money, and they didn't need a priest for that. 'Sorry, we've got bad news,' said one officer. 'We've found out that Paul and Neil have been killed in the Birmingham bombing.'

We didn't really understand politics back then, or the conflicts that were going on, but the police wanted us to help them. 'Look, work with us. Whatever happens with you getting sent to court, we can tell the judge to be a lot more lenient with you, if you start to give us information on the Irish people around here.'

We might have been in trouble, but we hated informers more than we hated the idea of going to prison. It didn't matter that whoever had committed the attack weren't allies to our gang. Snitching was the worst. We told the police to fuck off.

The accent was an interesting issue because of the politics of the time. In people's front rooms, little classes took place where tutors were helping Irish people to sound more Birmingham, to sound more *English*. They wanted to get rid of their Irish accents because it attracted police attention. Everybody was

under suspicion. Whenever people discussed what was going on with the accents, it was sometimes mentioned, 'Oh, this is what it was like back in the old days.' I didn't know what they were talking about then. It took *Peaky Blinders* to come along for me to understand.

So, there's always been a strong Irish community in Birmingham. There's always been a Republican community and they've always been under suspicion and under surveillance by the police. The police then came to the black gangs and the Rastafarians for help. They'd say, 'Look, we'll let you smoke your weed, if you just kind of give us some information on the Irish cats.' The response was always the same. We told them where to go. It was a plotline that wouldn't have looked out of place in *Peaky Blinders*.

The one question I get asked constantly is, 'Would there be a black person in Birmingham at that time?'

The answer is yes. Jimmy Jesus was a Jamaican guy who served alongside the boys from the Peaky Blinders in the First World War. For a while he returned home to Jamaica, but he missed his brothers from Birmingham so much that he moved there. While Jimmy was in the city, he slightly went off his head, later discovering that some of his old friends were gang members. He associated with the original Peaky Blinders but, as you know, the original Peaky Blinders weren't as big as they are in the programme.

His story later became the inspiration for Jeremiah Jesus. Becoming a preacher was easy for him. If you understand the Caribbean, then you know there's a church on almost every corner in Jamaica – I think they've got more churches per person than any other country in the world. It's only a small island, so you can understand why Christianity is so embedded in the people. It's not like an orthodox Christianity; it's the Christianity of our slave masters, actually – which is weird.

In Birmingham, Jeremiah turned into a preacher that, on one hand, wandered around, walking the streets of Birmingham, preaching death and fire to fornicators and thieves. At the same time, he was the eyes and ears of his fellow gang members on the street, because he knew what was happening; people came to him and they confessed their sins. He's definitely a wacky priest.

It's understandable that he might have been considered sectionable. Like Tommy, Arthur and the others, Jeremiah had only recently returned from the war, where life was brutal. There was real, hand-to-hand fighting. But doctors didn't recognize stress in the men coming home from France. There was a thing called shell shock, but that was only diagnosed if you completely lost it. But the stuff in between, the condition we now understand as PTSD, was not recognized. If you were functioning, if you were walking and off your head, like Jeremiah, then it didn't matter: it only mattered when you were completely incapable. Then you had shell shock and they locked you up in a home where you might receive electric shock therapy.

I love playing him. Something strange happens every time I go on set. When I put the clothes on, I slightly push my stomach out, to give me a bit more of a pot belly. I'm pretty flat-stomached, but I like to just push it out a bit; I stand in a slightly different way. We all do that: I watch Cillian when he dresses. As soon as he's got his gear on, he walks with his hands slightly out by his sides. And then Paul puts on a really growling Arthur voice: 'You going for dinner, Benjamin?' And he just goes into character straight away.

I remember when I was first doing it, I read the first words I had to speak, and I said, 'How do you want me to do this, Brummie or Caribbean, or what?' The director said, 'However you want to do it: don't come too heavy on the Caribbean, but don't overdo the Birmingham.' So the voice, especially when I'm preaching, is the same voice I use when I'm reading poetry live. It's a bit more Jamaican than my speaking voice. My speaking voice has become more English over the years. So, with the clothes on, my belly out, I look in the mirror and I know it's happened. It's usually when I put the hat on and the cross around my neck. That's it: I'm Jeremiah Jesus.

Jeremiah: Your sister and Freddie got back this morning. I tried following them, but Freddie is so good at hiding; he's like a fish.

Tommy: Right, well keep fishing.

I think the wedding between Tommy and Grace in Series Three is my favourite scene so far because it's slightly odd. I put on robes which reinforced the fact that I am a real priest. I'm not just pretending to be a priest; I'm a priest who's slightly nutty! There's a photograph of an out-take, when we weren't filming. It's me standing there, and Cillian and his bride-to-be were facing each other. Then Paul jumped in front of the camera, and put his thumbs up. The photo flew around the Internet! The church was full of people, supporting actors, and a lot of them were children. They all had to sing and it felt really inclusive, like a real wedding.

I feel very privileged in a way, because I'm the one person on the cast that's not a full-time actor. Some people have said, 'Why don't you have more of a role? Why are you not doing more?' I always say, 'Because I'm out on the streets, I'm in a world of my own; I'm not always hanging out with the Peaky Blinders, I'm going off, doing stuff …' That's especially so when the gang get money and move into their big houses. The idea was that Jeremiah could still be found on the street; I hadn't followed the Shelbys to their new life. I'm in Birmingham. When Tommy wants information, he comes back to me. He comes back to the street, where I whisper in his ear.

Jimmy Jesus wouldn't have been alone as a black man in Birmingham. There were others, it just wasn't a big community. I'm not sure if you'd call *Peaky Blinders* a period drama – I guess it's from the past, so maybe. But I've just noticed recently, since *Peaky Blinders,* that a lot more black actors are appearing in period dramas. I think *Peaky Blinders* was up there as one of the first. Jeremiah wasn't just a character for the sake it, he was a real character and wasn't token.

I hope Steve Knight is as proud of the role as me. For years I've frequented the little corners, and nooks and crannies of the city, so I really meet the people and I can see the pride it gives people from Birmingham: they love it. I support Aston Villa, but the Peaky Blinders are Blues (Birmingham City). So even when I go to games, they say, 'Benjamin, we still love you, even though you're a Peaky Blinder.'

But there are Blues fans that go to the games dressed as Peaky Blinders. There are a few characters in Birmingham who walk around there dressed as Peaky Blinders. But forget all that: the pride it's given people is huge, and it's not just the idea of, 'Oh, we've put ourselves on the map in Britain.' They know it's big around the world, too.

The other day, I got a script for something. Now, remember, I'm sixty years old. I don't call myself an actor, although I've been acting all through my life in a sense, doing different things, such

as poetry. But this script was just so stereotypical, in a negative way, of a black Rastafarian guy. I looked at it, and I just said, 'No.' I know *Peaky Blinders* is obviously about crime, but it's based on a reality. This programme comes in about black people in modern Britain and the script was me as a drug pusher and a gun seller; I'm asked to speak in a way that's not really the way we speak. I looked at it and I thought, 'Gosh, this is so dated.' I just couldn't believe somebody was sending it to me.

To do something that's reflecting a reality, like *Peaky Blinders* – though it is violent, and of course it's exaggerated, but it's rooted in some truth – makes me proud. It makes other people proud, like my mother, who says, 'Oh, it's a bit violent, but I love the way they talk about Small Heath and Washwood Heath and Alum Rock.' Places that we really know, rather than a stereotypical vision of London, or wherever. I'm very pleased with my role; I'm pleased with what the show has done – it's a snapshot of a fascinating period in British history, for so many different cultures.

The Heir Apparent

Finn Cole on Michael Gray

I first heard about the role of Michael Gray when my brother Joe, who plays John Shelby, told me there was a character in *Peaky Blinders* I might be able to play. I learned a bit more about Michael and thought, *Oh, yeah.* I was at college at the time, but it was obviously a great opportunity, one I had to jump at. We made a video on Joe's phone and sent it off to his agent. The next thing I know, I'm meeting with director Colm McCarthy, Series Two's casting director Shaheen Baig and Laurie Borg, the producer. I did a couple of readings for two different scenes and was offered the part. I couldn't believe it.

I was a huge fan of *Peaky Blinders,* firstly because Joe was in it. But I loved the show and I liked what they were doing; I really liked the stylistic and musical references they were using when creating the world the characters were moving within. And I loved the characters. Then suddenly I was on set, with my brother holding my hand through the making of Series Two, which was where Michael appeared for the first time as the estranged son of Polly. It was so helpful having him there. I could go onto a film set and ask stupid questions, like, 'Who does that?' Or, 'Where do we go for …?' It's quite a complicated place to be if you're not familiar with the set-up. Having Joe there to show me the ropes was great.

What really appealed to me with *Peaky Blinders* in that first series was the writing. Steve's knowledge of the characters and his research into Birmingham between the wars was beyond anything I'd seen before. I don't think anyone has beaten him in terms of quality when it comes to the stories he's trying to tell, and the characters that move within those tales. For an actor, what's great is that it allows us to interpret the events in our own way and sometimes do our own thing. That's how Paul Anderson really built up the character and emotion of his role. Steve's writing set the scene and Paul's used that to make the character even louder, even bigger and even stronger. It's very entertaining, because for a show that was possibly based all around one character – Tommy Shelby – Steve can now allow the responsibility to fall on other people's shoulders, which he's done with all of us.

When we meet Michael in Series Two, he's fresh-faced and innocent-looking, and it's a funny thing for actors when we get scripts like the ones given to us on *Peaky Blinders*. We don't really know what Steve has planned for us later on down the line; often the future of our characters is a mystery, but when I read the first few scenes that Michael was involved in I thought, 'I think I know where this is going …' He had the attributes to be a leader, to be in charge. He had those skills. The way Steve

We're not the Peaky fucking Blinders unless we are together.

Michael Gray

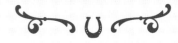

In my village there's this little wishing well. It's made of white bricks, right in the middle of the village green. Everybody says how pretty it is, but I swear to God, if I spend another day in that village I'm going to blow it up with dynamite. Probably blow my hands off with it, but it'll be worth it just to see those pretty white bricks all over the pretty village green.

Michael Gray

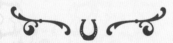

dropped those hints in the story was very subtle and it's a theme of Michael's character that has run through the entirety of the show. It's been very exciting to play that role.

As Steve first outlined the character to me, he described him as a younger version of Tommy. We discussed his ability to retain a cool, calm sense of control, but we also talked about his intelligence and his education. At times he could even be quite chilling – there was a lot of fun to be had in subtly mimicking Tommy at times. One of my favourite scenes involving him took place when Tommy and Michael first meet in Series Two. The pair of them are talking in a room together when Michael describes how there's a wishing well near to where he lives.

Michael is pressing upon Tommy the fact he hates where he's from; he wants to be a part of the Shelby family and it's his pitch to Tommy. He's saying he has it in him to step up – he has the gangster life in his blood. He's not just a kid that gets excited about the idea of the Peaky Blinders; he's serious, the gang's in his heart and that's only highlighted when Digbeth Kid, a character who names himself after Billy the Kid, much to the amusement of the gang, joins up. Digbeth's a bit childlike. The lads reckon he watches too many films and, in the end, the Sabini gang have him killed in prison.

It's a tragedy because he was just a wannabe. But it provides a nice contrast to Michael's arrival. He *isn't* a wannabe. He was born to be in that family and to be in that role. When he talks about the wishing well, Michael is telling Tommy, 'I'm ready for this.' It's a theme that's repeated later on when he says to Arthur and John that he's ready to kill Father John Hughes, after it's been revealed that, as a kid, he was once abused by the priest. He talks about how the gun feels like a part of his hand.

'How does it feel, Michael?' says John. 'Better than having a pen in your hand, innit? More like having your cock in your hand.'

Michael agrees. 'Yeah … Yeah, it does,' he says. It's a very powerful moment.

But his story is fascinating from the outset. Michael was a child in care, he was taken away when he was very young, but he's aware of his other family – he's aware that he's been adopted, but he's lived with a posh family for most of his life. When he meets Tommy, though, his life changes for ever. He sees this man; he has a dusty black coat and a red right hand, a character depicted by the Nick Cave & The Bad Seeds' song from the opening credits. To Michael's mind, Tommy is almost like a superhero: he's very impressive, very wealthy and he sees the potential for himself, if he were to follow the same path.

Immediately, Michael becomes aware that Tommy is lacking in empathy, which is something they both share. Michael's also lacking in a lot of sensitivity. Sure, he has charm and grace, but a lot of the emotional stuff a person needs to love and appreciate those people around him is missing. That makes Michael quite a dangerous person to be near, and a lot of the experiences he has as the series goes on only desensitize him further. When he goes to prison at the hands of Major Chester Campbell, in Series Two, he is abused in there by other inmates. We don't actually see it on screen and it's never explained explicitly to the audience, but the script notes for the character told of how he's been assaulted. On the day, a couple of lines were added to make it very clear that he had been raped in prison, but we weren't really sure if they were necessary. In the end we decided to suggest an idea instead, the notion of what *might* have happened to him. Michael had the shit beaten out of him by Campbell and his men and the attack toughens him up even more.

I think the source of this emotional detachment comes from the fact that Michael has never really experienced what real love is like. Because he's aware the family he's been living with aren't his flesh and blood – and he is under the impression that his real family didn't love him, and that his mother (Polly) didn't care – he develops an emotional armour. When he does eventually meet Polly, an interesting relationship builds between them because they're so similar. I often like to think that Michael's persona is a mix of Tommy and Polly. He has certain characteristics from both.

Certainly, he shares the experience of serious trauma, which so many of the Shelby family have gone through at one time or another. In Series Four he has two near death experiences: the first when he is shot in the same gun attack that kills John, and then when the Italian gangster, Luca Changretta, points a revolver at his face while he's recuperating in hospital. When he pulls the trigger there are no bullets loaded inside, thanks to a deal struck with Polly. Twinned with the fact he'd once been abused by Father John Hughes, all of those events have made him a very strong character and he's almost comfortable with the suffering he's experienced.

Also throw into that mix the sense he's very ambitious, that he likes success, and that he has plans ... it makes him very fun to play. He's also an addict, just like Tommy, but it's an addiction to power rather than drugs, or booze, that drives him, which I'm sure will be his downfall at some point. It catches up with him in Series Four when he doesn't tell Tommy about the news that the Italians have hatched a plan to assassinate the Peaky Blinders' leader, a plan made by Polly in order to save Michael's life, which is why he's eventually sent away to New York to expand the Shelby family business. But there's always been a ruthless streak in him. I'm interested to see what Steve does with the character; I'd like to think he's putting Tommy and Michael head-to-head in the long term.

When Michael sticks a knife into Father John Hughes's throat, it's a powerful moment for a number of reasons. The first is because nobody believes he has the nerve to go through with it at first, even though he tells the family, over and over, 'I can do this.' When he eventually does murder his abuser, Michael becomes even more comfortable in his darker self; he becomes a lot calmer and more in control as the story progresses, which I'd say makes him somewhat sociopathic. But I like that about

him. From the beginning of Series Two to the end of Series Three he transforms into a totally different character and the killing is a defining moment. It's an initiation into the other side of the family, which was what he'd wanted all along. Michael had been involved in the Shelbys' business, but he always wanted to work on the darker side, too.

Michael is so similar to Tommy and Polly, the two leaders of the family. All three of them operate in the same way, but they're so different at the same time. What he shares with both is their calm, cool and collected approach to confrontation. They also have the ability to win people over in a charming manner while completely taking control and making decisions. It's one of the reasons they have become so successful. What he doesn't have is the keen intelligence of Polly – she's a real thinker, while Tommy is more of a man, and I mean that in a negative way. There's something about women that run families or organizations. They have a better approach. They're more thoughtful. Tommy isn't like that.

Behind all the great families in crime dramas – and I say great even though we shouldn't be idolizing them – sit hugely powerful women who were actually mothers, or in Polly's case with Tommy, aunts. That's just how society has been throughout history; people like Polly haven't been named as the leaders of these families, but they make just as many decisions as everyone else. It's fascinating to me how Steve really makes that clear. Apparently, his mother was the same. From the stories he'd heard about the real Peaky Blinders gang, the women ruled the roost. A lot of the time, when the dads were in the pub, getting drunk and being actually quite nasty people, it was the women who raised the families. Not only that, but they'd also take responsibility for everyone in their neighbourhood. That was the story he wanted to tell and when you put that with an incredible performance from somebody like Helen, you have a fictional family that you want to follow and support.

The relationship with Michael and Polly has been fascinating throughout. I'm very close to my mother and the rest of my family, but to be in a unit that's as complicated as the Peaky Blinders is a very hard thing to put into words. I think that Michael has let Polly down a few times and he's done a few things that she doesn't necessarily agree with, but she's also absolutely in love with him. For a long time she thought he had been lost for ever and that she was never going to find him. Now he's back, she has someone to live for again, which makes her very protective of him throughout the story.

But that bond off screen helps to make us relatable on screen. No matter what the context of the story is – and it can be poetic, sexy and gruesome; it's very extreme and it's full-on. Whether that's Polly trying to stop Michael from doing something awful, or from Tommy and Arthur feuding about a familial decision, the audience still empathizes with the relationship between the individuals involved because they experience similar situations in their daily lives, just not with the same level of violence or criminality. The bonds are there, but the settings are different. It reflects the fact that there are ties within a family you won't have with anyone else outside of that group. I think a lot of families out there are tight; they have each other's back, always. It's nice to be able to see that in the Shelbys, too.

What the story represents is trust. It shows how a family will stay together under sometimes brutal and terrifying circumstances; they'll even take a bullet for one another. I think that's why *Peaky Blinders* is very enjoyable for so many people. Those characters on screen appear in every family, to a certain extent: there's someone who will take the pain for everyone else; there is someone who's in charge and another person who is more cool, calm and collected; there is someone that's not so smart and a little bit erratic, but also very emotional, and so on… A lot of people love a story about families because they can see where they might fit in within them.

Having my actual brother with me in the show was a particularly emotional experience, especially when his character is killed

*I've decided.
I want to make real
money. With you.*

Michael Gray

during an assassination by the Changretta gang in Series Four – an attack that almost sees Michael murdered, too. I was at the beginning of my career and I owed so much to Joe for getting me interested in the show and for helping me out with my role. In a way it was nice to be there and to watch him get shot on his last day, but it felt huge. What I love is that even after John's death, the other characters talk about him, there are photos of him everywhere and it's clear he hasn't been forgotten. It's a nice personal connection for me.

I'm fascinated to see where Michael's story will go as the *Peaky Blinders* plot continues. Steve has written a character with attributes that were plain to see from his very introduction. How he's fitted into the Shelby family set-up has been exciting to play and the personality has been fun to jump on board with. I often wonder, 'What can Steve do next?' The possibilities are endless, because he can make the stories work and he can make the characters so realistic. We get all six episodes before we start shooting – everything is planned, plotted and the series rarely changes as we begin filming. I love receiving those scripts and preparing for whatever's coming next. That's the most exciting part for me. I like reading the story of how Michael's rise to power is slowly but surely coming to life.

Always Within Punching Distance

Violence and vulnerability collide with devastating consequences for the Shelby family.

An Insider's Look at Series Three

From Tommy Shelby's mansion, the Peaky Blinders are fast approaching their 'existential crisis'. Having survived execution at the end of Series Two, and with his business empire expanding into American territories, Tommy is emboldened. His plan: to escape the criminal underworld his family have long inhabited while legitimizing their business concerns. Marrying Grace Burgess underpins his desire to leave a dark past behind; Tommy no longer wants to look over his shoulder for fear of attack and lurking in the shadows has become too troublesome. It's time for the Peaky Blinders to move on. But can they?

To capture the complex and emotional struggles in play, Belgian director Tim Mielants was brought in to helm all six episodes, having caught the eye with his 2014 drama, *Cordon* – the brooding story of a lethal virus outbreak in Antwerp. 'My understanding was that they wanted to have an evolution (from Series Two),' says Mielants. 'The swagger in Series Three is a little bit less than what we get in the previous series. There is a midlife crisis going on for these people. It's as if they're saying to themselves, "What are we doing? Are we going to do this for the rest of our lives?"

'They feel empty inside, a subject matter I really related to. Steve's writing was amazing. For me, the third series was a story of how power can lead to loneliness. Visually, we were very much inspired by films with a similar arc, such as *Citizen Kane*. How the big house starts to feel like a prison at the end. I don't get a lot of pleasure from Mafia, or swagger. It was interesting to give the show another layer, to take the story somewhere else.'

Through a nuanced story arc involving love, grief, betrayal and revenge, the key players in *Peaky Blinders* become even more multi-layered. Tommy Shelby's enemies have grown in numbers. Meanwhile, his marriage to Grace leaves him increasingly exposed to attack; it becomes common knowledge that Tommy's wife and new son, Charles, are his reachable points of weakness. As Major Chester Campbell discovered in Series Two, 'Tommy Shelby is not afraid to die.' And when a slow-burning feud with the Changretta crime family ignites following an assault by John on Angel Changretta, the attack blows back on Tommy with devastating consequences. An assassin murders Grace at a charity dinner and he emotionally unravels in the aftermath.

Initially, Cillian Murphy expressed doubts as to how best to play Tommy's character in a period of emotional despair. 'He wanted to know, "Should Tommy Shelby cry?"' said Mielants. 'And I said, "Yes, why not? Tommy has a wife and a child. It's the most vulnerable thing he can ever have in his life."

'Of course, he was a bit anxious about that. He'd been playing Tommy deadpan for two series, but because I'm a foreigner, because I related differently to the show, I said, "I feel we have to go there." Cillian is such a great actor and he managed to show a very interesting, vulnerable side of Tommy Shelby. We weren't quite sure what that would look like, but he was very proud of doing it in the end. It was something very beautiful.'

With Tommy's life in tatters, Murphy's emotional eloquence is ramped up even further. There's an intense guilt for Grace's death; Tommy knows the assassin's bullet was really meant for him, and to numb the pain he has a twisted affair with exiled Russian grand duchess, Tatiana Petrovna (Gaite Jansen). Together, they throw themselves into games of asphyxiation and Russian roulette, but intoxicated sexual release is not enough. As Tommy disconnects from his family, the Peaky Blinders become exposed.

Amid the emotional tumult, the gang becomes embroiled in a convoluted and dangerous plot to export weaponry and armoured vehicles, via train, to loyalist Russians fighting the Bolsheviks in Georgia. The plan is hatched through blackmail and financed by Petrovna's banished Russian aristocrats. Brokering the deal is the sinister Economic League, a far-right British political group who coerce Tommy, by threatening to reveal the Peaky Blinders' shadowy business enterprises. It's clear that the family will hang for their crimes should he refuse to complete the weaponry's safe passage.

The vilest characters

'Paddy has always been an actor we discussed for *Peaky*,' says casting director Shaheen Baig. 'Father John Hughes is a deeply complex character; he is really clever and utterly terrifying. I could watch Paddy read the phone book. There's a tense confrontation

in Series Three between Paddy and Cillian in the boatyard, where we had two actors who are at the top of their game, riffing off one another … It was fantastic. You wouldn't tell your confessions to Paddy in that vicar's outfit, would you?'

"I can charm dogs, and those I can't charm I can kill with my bare hands."

— Tommy Shelby

A series of switches and double-crosses take place. The Russian aristocrats initially plan to pay the Peaky Blinders in jewellery for transporting the weaponry – stones and Fabergé eggs brought into England and stashed in a shadowy vault under the Thames. (To prove their trust, they had gifted Tommy a sapphire, which was later revealed to be cursed; Grace was murdered with the trinket dangling around her neck.)

However, the scheme is manipulated from the outset. The Economic League have a secret plan: details of the shipment are leaked to Soviet forces who endeavour to destroy the cargo train with the Peaky Blinders still on board, in the process committing an atrocity on British territory. Tommy learns this has been the Economic League's intentions all

along: their hope is for the British government to sever ties with the Soviet Union during the political fallout, and when the Peaky Blinders learn of their role as collateral damage, they work with the communists to sabotage the shipment. But Father Hughes remains on their tail at every turn, his on screen persona delivering both malevolence and menace.

'He was possibly the vilest character that Steve ever created,' says Cillian Murphy. 'Paddy did such a brilliant job and he's such a darling man, a wonderful man, but he managed to imbue Father Hughes with such horror, it's beyond thinking.'

'I directed him in a surreal way and Paddy liked it,' says Mielants. 'He was so confident in himself, and he patronized the other characters. We had the same memories of teachers from high school. I remember us sharing memories of the way people patronized kids in the class, so we based him on that. Father John Hughes likes to be surrounded by high-class people – he finds that pleasant. Those two elements were interesting: the patronizing guy, and the guy who feels good in high society.'

When the Peaky Blinders later rob the Russian's safe, they give the loot to Grand Duchess Tatiana Petrovna in exchange for cash; the value of the haul was assessed by jewellery expert Alfie Solomons, a character who proves duplicitous throughout the show.

'The sequence in the safe was really nice because my idea was to give him a lamp so he could study the jewellery. I wanted him to hold something. I said, "Let's do the lighting by giving him the lamp and letting him walk around the room." We went through the scene beat by beat. I loved the energy. The whole thing took twenty-five minutes, just on set. We played the whole scene through every time and we did it five or six times, but always from a different angle. It felt like a play. That feeling came across on screen.'

Cherchez la femme

Amid the chaos, Arthur Shelby, a broken man stripped bare by PTSD, cocaine abuse and uncontrollable violence, finds solace in his new partner, Linda. A Quaker, her religious beliefs arrive at the right time for a personality on the brink. Arthur turns to God in order to extract himself from a lifestyle he knows is tipping him towards self-destruction, but as Linda becomes pregnant, the couple eventually impact upon one another. Linda tussles with Tommy, negotiating a better pay deal for Arthur. She then cajoles the Shelby girls into joining a women's strike organized by union trouble starter, Jessie Eden (Charlie Murphy).

'Off screen, in between Series Two and Three, it was Tommy's idea to get a Christian woman to calm Arthur down,' says Steven

Knight. 'But I wanted to play with the thought that, while Linda converts him to religion, he converts her to the way of his family. Linda loves it. She loves that life and gets addicted to it.

'Historically, the Quakers built a whole suburb on the south side of Birmingham called Bourneville, where the chocolate was made. The Quakers understood alcohol was a big problem in the area, and in the Bourneville district there were no pubs. What they foolishly believed was that they could open cafes instead, where they sold hot chocolate. They thought that chocolate was the virtuous pleasure instead of alcohol, which is why Cadbury, Fry's and Rowntree's were all originally Quaker families from the Midlands. I wanted someone from that background to try to grab Arthur and save him.'

For Polly, her position becomes even more precarious than in previous series. The reunion with her son, Michael, in Series Two, has turned bittersweet as he is drawn closer to the Peaky Blinders' violent orbit. When she learns that Michael plans to murder Father John Hughes, after it's revealed the priest abused him while in foster care, she even warns the family: 'I swear to God, if Michael pulls the trigger, I will bring this whole fucking organization down around your ears.' Under Steven Knight's narrative, Michael's personality, which chilled dramatically throughout Series Two, takes a more sinister turn. And Polly is powerless to stop him.

'It's always interesting to look at people who can cope with their emotions, almost like psychopaths,' says Steven Knight. 'That was something we played with. I could tell Finn Cole was a great talent.'

As her son becomes increasingly imperilled, Polly tries to make her escape from a life that now terrifies her, yet she makes a series of clumsy, and sometimes dangerous, missteps. During confession, she inadvertently mentions that the Peaky Blinders have a 'man of the cloth' in their sights. Father Hughes is alerted to their plans to kill him and moves on the Shelbys before they have a chance to strike. Tommy is hospitalized in a brutal assault by the priest's men. And Father Hughes later kidnaps

Charles with the aim of forcing Tommy to blow up the train himself.

'The confession scene is the core of what Polly is all about,' says Mielants. 'We see her deeper side. I experienced Helen's true talent there. For a director, it was like somebody giving me the keys to an extremely good car – it does whatever you want. As she reveals everything to Father Hughes we see that Polly is stuck in a prison she can never get out of.

'Helen knows a lot about the English class system. She's very aware of that and she explained what it was like to me, as a foreigner, how freeing yourself from the world you're living in is extremely difficult. I could relate to that because my parents came from a working-class background in Antwerp.

They had been studying and they tried to go somewhere higher. We used that idea together in every scene.'

Even Polly's romantic tryst with the artist Ruben Oliver – who paints her portrait – turns briefly sour when Tommy reveals that the Peaky Blinders' plans to rob the Russians has been betrayed. Tommy accuses Oliver of the double-cross and Polly destroys her portrait in a fury, confronting the artist by pointing a gun at his head. (It later turns out to be Alfie Solomons.) 'With Ruben, Polly tries to be someone else,' says Mielants. 'A normal woman with a normal life and normal ambitions. But she finds out that she isn't normal. She's one of the guys.'

As the train plot reaches a furious boiling point, Series Three's close is both tangled and adrenalized. Polly is powerless to protect her son and Michael, driven by revenge, eventually kills Father Hughes. Despite his death and Charles' safe passage home, there is no time to abort the train attack – the news arrives too late. The train is blown to smithereens, and innocent railway workers are killed.

The pull of the Peaky Blinders

With the gang reconvened at the Shelby mansion, Tommy hands over several wads of cash as payment for the gang's completed mission, railing against his naive plans to shoulder the Establishment. 'I've learnt something in the last few days: those bastards are worse than us,' he shouts. 'Politicians, lords and ladies, they're all worse than us and they will never admit us to their palaces, no matter how legitimate we become because of who we are and where we're from.'

As Arthur and Linda reveal their intention to open a grocery store in California, the mood sours further. 'You can go, but you won't get far, Arthur,' says Tommy. 'I spoke to (Sergeant) Moss last night. He told me that the Chief Constable of Birmingham has issued a warrant for your arrest: murder, sedition, conspiracy to cause explosion.

'John, they're coming for you as well: murder, sedition, conspiracy to cause explosion. Michael: the murder of Hughes. Polly: the murder of Major Campbell. The people we betrayed last night, they control the police, they control the judges; they control the jails. But they do not control the elected government. Listen to me; I have made a deal in return for giving evidence to them. It's all taken care of.'

Police officers bang on the mansion doors. The Shelby family are heading for the gallows, their futures in the balance. Despite the best efforts of an emotionally and physically damaged leader, escape from their class and criminality has proved impossible.

'The question of the whole show is, *Can you escape?*' says Steven Knight. '*Can you get away from your roots in England?* Ada is the first one to try in Series One, but she's pulled back. Arthur tries in Series Three and gets pulled back. Polly tries and gets pulled back. Tommy is the centre of the orbit and the others are constantly dragged back in.

'Tommy says it in Series Three at the end in his speech; *you'll never be accepted.* And it's the truth. In the story he later receives an OBE, but it doesn't mean a thing. But in Series Three, Tommy decides he doesn't give a fuck. He thinks, *The Establishment are worse than us and we have to carry on …*'

For Mielants, the final scene was an experience that drew together several months of intense work. 'I was thinking, "OK, here's when it all comes together."' As the cast and crew read through the script, Helen McCrory suggested the family should embrace Arthur

as he announces his plans to emigrate. 'That was a great addition,' says Mielants. 'It worked almost immediately – it was very strange. I remember Cillian sitting next to me saying, '*Fuck.* This is working …' You have to get lucky sometimes and we got lucky there.

'I worked so hard, almost all year, all the time, and it was all *Peaky* – I had nothing else in my life. I went very deep. It was a beautiful experience and it did something beautiful with the audience, and that makes me happy.'

Superstition

STEVEN KNIGHT: Superstition and black magic has played a part in *Peaky Blinders* from the very first scene of Series One, when Tommy pays a Chinese fortune-teller to blow a 'magic' red dust on the horse, Monaghan Boy, as he walks it through the streets of Small Heath. The spell is supposed to bless the animal before it later races at Kempton Park.

By Series Three, Tommy uses superstition to ease his guilt and grief over Grace's death at the hands of the Changrettas at a charity party. Before her murder, a sapphire is given to him as payment for his killing of Russian spy Anton Kaledin (Richard Brake), which he later gives to Grace. After the assassination, Tommy comes to believe that the stone is cursed. He visits the Gypsy Bethany Boswell (Frances Tomelty) for confirmation.

Here, Tommy is using superstition for a very practical reason. He's saying, 'Grace's death is not my fault. Tell me that her death is not my fault and this is cursed, and I'll feel better.' It's a logical and practical approach to superstition. The line I'm most pleased with is when Tommy says, 'All religion is a foolish answer to a foolish question.' I think what the storyline does is present us with some profound ideas about religion and culture.

I'm interested in Gypsy culture, where there is a lot of superstition and belief in spirits, but also in ways of telling the future. The old circus method of working with superstition was a way of making money with con tricks, but there was also a belief in what was considered to be the real thing. A lot of that faith was introduced to me by my mum. She was quite superstitious, but the idea underpinning this theme is that Tommy is the most practical man. Yet he also believes in superstition. He feels you shouldn't mess with it.

That was a common idea with people who dealt with horses. My dad and my brother – who is still a blacksmith – took on the trade and they can communicate with horses

somehow; the horses somehow communicate with them. There was also the idea in my family that dreams could indicate the future. My mum was a big believer in that. There was also a lot of folklore regarding the properties of certain objects, good and bad. Sometimes, Dad would 'find things before they were lost', but my mum stopped him from bringing one or two items into the house because they were considered to bring bad fortune.

I researched the superstitious elements from the show through my own background. I don't really trust books for information on Gypsy culture – they're not that accurate. The ideas I used were bits and pieces I picked up as a kid; the things you were supposed to do and not do; the idea of luck and what can be done to bring good luck while avoiding bad

luck. I'm still really superstitious. There are certain feathers I wouldn't have in the house and certain feathers I will.

We continue the theme of superstition into Series Five. A Gypsy places a drop of blood into a bowl of water. When she touches it, the blood ripples, allowing the person to see the future. This was a real practice called 'scrying'. It's fascinating stuff and visually great. It really adds to the look of the show.

The women's strike

TIM MIELANTS: For this scene, I had the female members of the Shelby family walking down the street, and was thinking of *The* *Right Stuff*, the Mercury space program movie where NASA astronauts walk side by side to the rocket launch. I wanted them walking next to each other and to make them swagger as much as they could. That was the way we tried to do it, but we wanted to make it slightly too swaggering. There was a fine line because I was not reaching for a laugh, I was reaching for a sense of, *'This is cool.'*

The music was really important because for the first time we were putting some female swagger into the show. And the actors had a lot of fun. Helen's glasses were incredible but it was very hard for me when deciding where to put Polly in the line-up. At first, I put Polly

in the middle but it didn't quite work, so I had the idea of putting her on the right side. I'd remembered a theory in politics that, because we read from left to right, the strongest person should be on the right because that's the end of the sentence. That's where you land. I don't know if there was truth in it, but it worked out very well.

STEVEN KNIGHT: Jessie Eden was a real person. There's less of her in Series Five, but she returns with a vengeance. She was based on a woman who was in her early twenties, and the real Jessie Eden was a shop steward from the Lucas factory in Birmingham in the 1920s. She brought out all the women in a strike at the Lucas factory, which made electrical machinery. That's the labour dispute I refer to when Lizzie and Polly join the strike in Series Three.

Jessie Eden eventually went to live in Russia and came back, organizing rent strikes and other social protests into the 1960s. I wanted to get her in because, having read about her, I realized how opposite she was to Tommy. I've always had in mind that Tommy would eventually be genuinely redeemed. All the things he sets up, like charities and foundations, he does it for a superficial purpose but eventually they will become legitimate.

By the end of the *Peaky Blinders* story, Tommy will genuinely become a good man and Jessie Eden is a part of that change. Tommy uses her in Series Four and he's not genuine, but as we go into Series Five and he confronts fascism, he thinks, 'Well, maybe there is virtue.' Jessie Eden represents that virtue. When we had the premier for Series Four, Jessie Eden's adopted son and his wife came along. Luckily, they loved the show, they loved the depiction and thought it was fantastic.

Part Four

My Suits Are on the House

Hair pomade and razor blades: inventing
the look of *Peaky Blinders*.

How the Look of *Peaky Blinders* Came to Be

When Paul Anderson, the actor responsible for bringing the reckless physicality of Arthur Shelby to *Peaky Blinders*, attended a Halloween party in 2018, he was greeted with an unusual sight. Dressed as the Hollywood depiction of H. G. Wells's famous character, the Invisible Man, Anderson was surprised to see several guests dressed in flat caps, heavily tailored suits and clumpy boots. Each outfit had been offset with a fake moustache. Evidently, the in-look that year was the very character immortalized on screen by Anderson since 2013.

'They never noticed me,' he says. 'I was wrapped in bandages, with a suit and a Trilby hat on. So I walked past these two geezers who were dressed up as Arthur and said, 'Who have you come as, mate?' One of them replied, 'You don't know who this is? I'm Arthur fucking Shelby! *By order of the Peaky Blinders*!' When I counted, there were six of them in the room. Some of the looks were terrible.'

Such is the astonishing impact of *Peaky Blinders*' intricately constructed, and expertly researched, sartorial design. Six years on from its launch, the show's influence on modern fashion has been undeniable, particularly within men's styling. Hair salons offer 'The Peaky Cut'. High-street retailers dress their windows with mannequins draped in tapered trousers, penny-collar shirts, tweed overcoats and heavy, but stylish, leather boots. David Beckham's style brand, Kent & Curwen, have even unveiled a range of clothes and flat caps under the 'Garrison Tailors' brand, an official collaboration with the producers of *Peaky Blinders*.

Elsewhere, established style bibles have spent five years pulling together guides on how best to capture the 'definitive *Peaky Blinders* look'. And as the dresses and hairstyles of characters such as Polly Gray and Ada Thorne became increasingly elegant – the Peaky Blinders crime family advancing in power and wealth on screen – fashion blogs detail the behind-the-scenes creativity responsible for their opulent appearances. Details on how certain materials had been

embroidered with threads made from silk and metal, and offset with crystal and Miyuki beads, became the focus of online think pieces.

Many of *Peaky Blinders*' design elements are rooted in historical context. When Steven Knight first drew up plans to write a western-styled drama based in 1920s Birmingham, his hope was to give its characters a larger-than-life vibe. One way of ensuring this mood was to arm its protagonists with lavish clothes and striking haircuts. 'Someone referenced the Brian de Palma film, *The Untouchables*,' says executive producer Jamie Glazebrook, 'and how that film was set in the 1920s, or 30s, but the clothes they wore in the film were quite 1980s. There was always the intention to make *Peaky Blinders* not feel so period-y.'

The final designs, however, were much more than a contemporary flight of fancy. 'People looked fantastic then,' says Steven Knight. 'The gangsters spent all their money on clothes. The *Peaky Blinders* era was all about having an older look, looking like men, rather than kids. You would get your first suit when you were fifteen and you would hope to have it for ten years.'

The suits, such as those worn by Cillian Murphy, were designed by Savile Row tailor Keith Watson. 'The boys loved their clothes,' says costume designer Stephanie Collie from Series One. 'I think you get a feel of that by the way they walk; they have a swagger about them.' Though one chilling addition to the *Peaky Blinders*' clobber might have heightened that sense of bravado. Among the dandy styling and intricate detailing, razor blades were stitched into flat caps worn by Anderson, Murphy and Joe Cole. The real-life gang was even reputed to have drawn its name from this gore-splattering design.

This twist has caused some controversy, however. Having been dramatized in Series One, the suggestion of gangsters wielding weaponized headwear was disputed by some people. Knight remains convinced of its authenticity. 'There were razor blades,' he says. 'Some people have said that people went around each other's house for a cup of sugar in those days. That it was all lovely and there was no crime; the idea that, "Yeah, we all went to the corner shop for sweets …"

'It has been claimed the Peaky Blinders never wore razor blades in their caps. But I know that my aunties and uncles told me that they *did* put in razor blades and they did it in Glasgow. They even put razor blades in their lapels. They were stitched all the way down, so if somebody grabbed at a Peaky Blinder's jacket, the blades would slice their assailants' hands to ribbons. The gangsters would strike at somebody and put the cap back on. It was the same in London: the razor blade was the weapon of choice.'

As the plot has progressed and characters such as Tommy make strides into increasingly legitimate business practices, so their outfits match a sense of escalating social ambition. Suits become more intricately constructed. Research into the dresses, shoes and accessories of *Peaky Blinders* focused on Hollywood movies made in the early twentieth century. 'There was a lot of exploration for women in the twenties,' says Alison McCosh (costume designer, Series Four and Five). 'I think we've really captured that in Polly Gray's looks. It's important to listen to the actors and what they want for their characters, as well as realizing the writer's vision. I wanted Polly to come forward with her costumes, so she has a lot of colour. I went to Italy and the US to source materials and fell in love with a little bit of fur, as well as some intricate lace for Helen's costumes.

'As they are so delicate and of the period, we had to reinforce some of the dresses, so that they could last the length of the shoot. But that's the beauty of the role: to preserve the dresses. We're committed to it and we love it.'

As production begins with every new series of *Peaky Blinders*, the work on set takes up a familiar rhythm. Scripts are delivered. Read-throughs are organized. But when the cast gather together for rehearsals, one routine tends to bring their roles into sharper

focus: hair-styling sessions. Curls are teased into 'fuzzy Gypsy' flourishes; heads shaved uncomfortably close to the skull. But when the show's distinctive looks were first unveiled for Series One in 2013 – solely devised by hair and make-up designer, Laura 'Loz' Schiavo – there was a brief period of discontent. Schiavo even recalls Joe Cole's horror as his hair was shaved down to nothing.

'Poor Joe Cole,' says Schiavo. 'He sat in my chair and had no clue. He came in with glasses and brown hair. He walked out with skin, his first Peaky Cut on top. I dyed it, too. All the boys, when they saw it, said, "*Oh, fuck.*" Otto was like, "Oh yes! *This is what I'm talking about.*" Otto had told me, "I want someone who won't do normal haircuts." I don't do anything normal – I go completely off-piste all the time. As a stylist, as long as I'm not bringing the future into it, I can do whatever I want.

'And I wanted a haircut where, when the boys have their hats on, all you see is the skin around the backs and sides of the head.

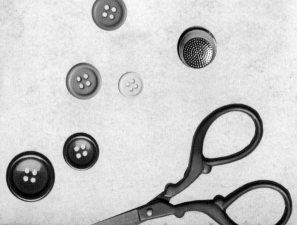

And when they take their hats off, you see an individual hairstyle for each person. There was also a book called *Crooks Like Us* (2009) – by Peter Doyle, on criminals from 1920s Sydney – that was a major inspiration.'

Strangely, in the following eighteen months, the haircut became a twenty-first-century style phenomenon, known by stylists as the 'Peaky Cut'. 'It was partly inspired by hygiene,' says Cillian Murphy. 'People were infested by lice in the First World War.'

The look later became a dramatic tool in times of violence. With their caps removed, fists and razor blades flying, the fringes of Murphy, Anderson and Cole flailed around with striking effect. 'When they did go in with the razor, their hair flicked forward,' says Schiavo. 'We did a great fight scene on the Gypsy site in Series One and it was brilliant.' Other characters were later given a more nuanced style, she explains. 'Tommy Shelby's hair was always severe but it became very sharp and smarter as his business interests drifted into the right side of the law. I like changing the boys' hair every series, too – mixing it up. New addition to the Peaky Blinders gang, Michael Gray, was presented in a way that placed him on the peripheries of mob life.

'I talked about it with the director and Cillian and we worked out that Michael's not really a true Peaky. He has an underlying idea that he'd *like* to be a Peaky, but he's not really. So we kept his hair very short and smart; a typical 1920s haircut. That was our thing: Michael becomes the accountant, he's not the one that goes out and kills. He's not the gangster. That's why we didn't go that way. I threatened him with it though …'

For the female cast members, their hairstyles have evolved through fashion and circumstance. Lizzie Stark has travelled from part-time prostitute to established figure within the Shelby family. 'Her hair should look neat all the time, quite proper. I gave her the really low parting on one side. And her hair was a lot more chic.' Ada's move from Birmingham to America gives her a look that's more on trend for the era. 'The Peaky girls have got a lot of money and the Garrison women are more street,' says Schiavo. 'They're not from a lot of money, so you have to show the class differences between the Peaky ladies and the Garrison ladies. The hair can really change a character. Ada goes to America, comes back, and she's got to be a hot chick.'

Polly Gray's progression from gangster totem to vulnerable mother on the cusp of madness was depicted through a series of styles: at first, Gypsy leader, then she was later transformed into a look that recalled several silver-screen heroines of 1920s Hollywood. 'In Series Four, Polly goes a bit mad,' says Schiavo. 'So when she gets out of prison at the beginning, she has the haircut from a year previously. Then we see her in her house. Time has gone by and her hair has grown long. She's thinking, "I don't give a stuff about anything," and she doesn't care about being a Peaky Blinder, hence she lets her hair grow longer. Then she suddenly snaps out of it and thinks,

"Right, I want to be a Peaky." That's when we decided to give her short hair. I gave her a wig and cut it into a short crop style for Series Four. In Series Five, her hair is longer, curlier and sexier – again, that's a wig.

'I can see actors' personalities change once they get their haircut. They turn into their character. It really changes them a lot. Cillian especially, it alters his whole face shape. It's amazing; it's transformative. The very moment he has the haircut, Cillian *is* Tommy. Paul *is* Arthur. And it sets them out to be completely different.'

Helen McCrory on the style of Polly Gray

Series One director Otto Bathurst came to my house and said, 'Right, this is the reason you've got to do *Peaky Blinders* …' And he was so precise about the way everybody looked. He is a dandy himself. Otto wears beautiful clothes and hats. He's an extraordinary dresser, so he was very exact about all the costumes.

I knew that Polly was very tightly wound as a character; she was *coiled*. By that I mean that it takes a long time for Polly to understand when she's safe, and she never feels safe. She's an alley cat. She's always ready. You sense that Polly could pack her bag in fifteen minutes to flee the country. That's what I mean by coiled.

To get that idea on screen I said, 'All my clothes: I want them to be hobbled skirts. I want my corset, from the top to the bottom, to be brought in. I want scarves. I want hats. I want gloves half a size too small for my hands. I want my shoes to have tiny little buttons all the way up to my knees. It all has to be coiled. *She* has to be coiled …'

Otto was great because he absolutely

understood what I was doing and encouraged all my exactness. Some directors don't really care what the actresses wear. They're more interested in talking about something else. But Otto understood the look of Polly. The first scene I did was where I walked down the cobbled streets of Garrison Lane and met John, whacking him across the head, snarling, *'Get off your arse, you mumping pig!'* We'd shot that scene for forty minutes, in sleet and rain. My wool was so heavy, I squelched when I walked onto the set.

I wanted Polly to be coiled because when I first asked Steve who she was, he replied, 'Well, Tommy Shelby is the man that's going to run the gang. But behind every man there will be a woman. That's where Polly comes in.' I knew she had to be tough, especially if Polly was telling the men what to do and they were fucking doing it.

But it's not just a physicality that Polly has when she's knocking somebody around the back of the head with a gun. It's also wisdom and that Gypsy quality of hers. Steve has given her a sensitivity – not a second sight – that's very familiar to a lot of women. The women that often say, 'I just felt it.' Or, 'I knew it.' Polly's also got a wit. She whiplashes people's arses with a funny line, or put-down. In every scene, I often have a little gun on my person. You can't see it, it's held in my stocking and garter. Even though I never use it, I still wear it because I walk in a slightly different way when I've got a gun strapped to my thigh.

Polly can set a mood by adjusting her hairpin. Now she's gone up in the world financially, she has one stuck into a fox fur, which she wears over her shoulders. But what's so much fun is the inventiveness of it all. Those costume details aren't in the script.

That's a decision made by myself and the costume designer. Alison McCosh (Series Four and Five) is the most talented costume designer you'll ever work with. She sources Polly's costumes from all over the world: museums, collections. Before we start filming, the actresses are sent photographs of fifteen outfit choices, all of which have hats, gloves and shoes to match. It's whatever we fancy. She's a real artist. And when I'm being styled by Loz Schiavo, she makes Polly's hair frizzy, like it would have been back then. It's fun to put the Vaseline on the eyelids, the kohl around the eyes. It's a completely different look to how women wear make-up today. It brings an authenticity and a griminess.

And that's what I like about *Peaky*. I like the griminess.

The hair has been fantastic. Women are supposed to complain about what they look like when they're on set, but there have been very few grumbles. And once the men realized, three years later, that all of Hoxton Square were sipping their mochaccinos with the same *Peaky Blinders* haircut, they realized it wasn't so bad.

I put a lot of thought into the details of Polly's outfits. There's a costumiers in London called Cosprop, and I go there before the start of every job I do. I basically go through the place and find all the things I need. I was the one who found Polly's hatpins. I found the keys to put around her waist; I find Bibles, I find rosaries. Before the second series, when Polly discovered her daughter was dead, I went to a

market and bought two beautiful, carved baby toys. I had them in the locket around my belt for the entire series. You never saw them, but they were there to have.

There's so much inventiveness in *Peaky Blinders*. And that's so much fun.

The *Peaky Blinders* look, by the cast

FINN COLE: It's actually the haircut that really gets me into character. I start to feel totally different as soon as that's done. I'm so aware of it, and the style that Loz has put together really signifies the *Peaky Blinders* for me. Although I don't have the full chop, it was definitely the haircut that finished off the look: it's very clean, there's lots of pomade and it's slicked back. The mad thing is there are so many people on the streets wearing that haircut. It's seriously popular.

PAUL ANDERSON: I never liked it; I hated it in fact. I questioned why, constantly. It was Otto Bathurst's idea, credit to him, and Steve Knight. When you read about the Peaky Blinders, there's one page on Google and their outfits sounded terrible. They wore flared trousers, bell-bottom trousers and hobnailed boots. We changed that and turned them into bespoke, tailor-made suits and sharp haircuts. But those haircuts existed in the twenties.

The haircut looks good, but to actually wear that haircut, to have it in my everyday life, was different at first. I didn't mind it on set, but when I came back to London, and I walked through the West End with that haircut, I felt too trendy. Even though I could carry myself and I like to think I dress well, I'm certainly not as far as that into fashion, or what's on trend.

CILLIAN MURPHY: I think the look was quite common, not just in Britain, but in America, as well. For these working-class lads, any money they'd earn, they spent it on tailoring, just to make themselves sharper. It was the only way to glamorize the pretty shitty existence that they had. We've taken that look and really, really pushed it and heightened it. The haircuts were absolutely laughed at – I'd

be walking along and people would stop on the street and laugh at me. Now everyone's wearing them and voluntarily asking for a *Peaky Blinders* haircut.

We get to wear beautifully tailored suits. Any man who's had the pleasure of having a suit tailored for him, as opposed to buying one off the rail, can tell the difference; it's like wearing a glove. When that glamour and tailoring is juxtaposed against that grime of an industrial Birmingham, it looks great. The silhouette of the peaked cap and the long coat and the tailored suit was quite cool, instantly.

The Feral Princess

Sophie Rundle on Ada Thorne

When Steve Knight first described the character of Ada Thorne to me, he said, 'She should be feral. She's the only girl among the Shelby family. Her aunt Polly is the matriarch, but Ada's the only girl and she's just as smart as Tommy, and just as fearless as the rest of the Shelbys. She has a different agenda and a different way of thinking a lot of the time, but she's a full-blooded Shelby, whether she wants to be or not.'

I loved that. I've never had someone tell me that a character was feral growing up, especially a female character. There's a softer side to Ada too, and I saw a lovely thing on Instagram where someone described her as 'The Princess of Birmingham'.

I've always enjoyed the idea that the Shelbys were the royal family of the city, but they're more rock 'n' roll. I constantly wonder what Ada is going to be like when she's a grandma. God, imagine: Grandma Ada and the stories she'd tell of her 1920s life in a gangster set with her wild and lawless brothers.

The idea of Ada's toughness was summed up in the finale of Series One. The Peaky Blinders are going head-to-head with Billy Kimber's gang in a Wild West-style showdown, but Ada barges between the two warring groups with her kid, Karl, ordering the mobs to pack it in. That was mad! The crew told me their plans for the scene and because I was so new I became a little nervous. 'Oh, no,' I thought. 'I've got to do this speech in front of all the cast …' But it was a brilliant image: Ada, pushing her pram through a scrum of gangsters with guns, positioning herself in the middle of the shoot-out. She's unfazed because she's grown up with this stuff. It holds no fear for her. It's rare that you get to play a woman like that in this game. I love Steve for it.

All of the women are strong in Steve's story, though. I think that's something people love about *Peaky Blinders:* anybody who comes from a family recognizes that, more often than not, it's the women who are in charge. Or, the women can be as scary as the men. That's what Steve has really cottoned on to. Sure, we have characters like Tommy and Arthur. Everyone is a gun-slinging cowboy. But the women are just as tough and I think that makes them so exciting.

I love Ada for her amazing journey. I've grown up with the show and I've grown up with her. She's definitely done her teenage rebellion years. In Series One when she marries the communist and union agitator, Freddie Thorne, she knows that pisses off her older brother, Tommy. With all that wild feral energy she possesses as a Shelby, Ada doesn't do anything by halves.

The family go with their hearts, secretly, really, deep down. I think they're *emotional* people, and that's why we love them. They're not simply cold-hearted monsters.

Ada later dips her toe into politics. She goes around the

We're a close family – always within punching distance.

Ada Thorne

houses rebelling against everything and then she goes back into the Shelby fold during Series Four. I love the fact that she's not frightened of her family. She'll say, *'I don't care if you're the Peaky Blinders, you can do one!'* Then she often realizes that there's no escape from where she's come from, like so many of the characters in the story. The Shelbys and their past will always be part of her, so maybe it's better to lean into them, their way of life, and embrace her reality. Throughout it all, Ada sticks with her people, she sticks with her tribe.

That's been her journey from the very beginning. I still can't believe I got the job.

It was one of my first roles out of drama school. I was clueless, but I think that helped because, when I sent the tape through, the casting directors said something like, *Just tape for whatever role you want to tape for. Any of the female parts …* Obviously I went for Ada because she's the coolest person in the world. I did the tape and went for it.

I think I had really dodgy hair at that time. It was dyed. I was just out of drama school and I had no money, what with being a student, and I'd done a self-styling job. I'd originally wanted a very glamorous shade of dark brown but it turned black, so I showed up to my audition with this jet-black hair. I looked ridiculous. I made out that I'd meant it to be rock 'n' roll and cool, but it was absurd. Still, it kind of worked for Ada, especially in Series One because she *was* a total rock star.

I remember when we were making Series One; I was so new. Everyone around me was saying, 'God, I think *Peaky Blinders* is going to be really special, because it's so *different* …' I just assumed that all jobs were like that. I thought it was ever going to be thus, for everything I did. It's only now that I can see quite how amazing that first series was.

Imagine meeting Helen McCrory on your first job. Someone described her to me as being 'minty', which was so brilliant. She was already one of my heroes when I went into the show and she took the part of Polly Gray and ran with it. I think it's because of

Oi! I'm a Shelby too, you know. Put my fucking film back on!

Ada Thorne

people like Cillian Murphy and Paul Anderson, and Helen that the show is what it is. We watch them on set and love them, but the ideas they bring to their performances, and the things they throw out there that aren't on the page: it's what's so inventive and so mad about *Peaky Blinders*.

But the show is *completely mad*. It has such a fierce sense of its own identity because of people like Cillian and Helen and Paul, and everybody shows up on every series with so much enthusiasm. Helen is fearless, which is so intrinsic to Polly, but she's also got this deep vulnerability to her, which is why we love Polly. Paul is scary as Arthur, but he's a teddy bear really. It's why we love all the characters. They've all got that human strand. They're all trying to make their way in life and their struggles are visceral.

Motherhood changes Ada drastically. She becomes more protective. She grows up. When we first meet her in Series One she's a teenage gangster brat, but the birth of Karl alters her in the way that motherhood alters every woman. Also, the death of Freddie impacts her massively. She really grieves, taking herself off from her family when she moves to London, which is a massive step. Ada is a young single mum, a situation that forces a person to adapt fast.

Ada is no different and toughens up. She matures by being a mother and by having seen behind the curtain of what Tommy and Polly are doing to keep the Shelby family together, and what they have to do to protect the family. She gathers a keener understanding of those challenges, and because of that her bond with Polly becomes even stronger.

Ada's relationships with her brothers are just as interesting. She loves the bones of Arthur; she thinks he's as mad as a box of frogs. Ada and Arthur are completely different people, but they love each other and their worlds don't collide a huge amount. With Tommy, it's different. He traverses into politics and the higher echelons of society, which are the worlds that Ada has always wanted to get into, so it's natural there's a connection between them there. Tommy is her weakness; as is the rest of the family, which is why Ada always goes back to them throughout the story. What she wants at first is to completely ostracize herself and run away from her past. In Series Two she wants to join the Bloomsbury set in London because she is whip-smart – she understands philosophy, art and politics. She reads a lot.

In a different world she would have gone to university and been the badass CEO of some very high-powered company. But she can't reject her family for too long because she loves them too much – it would be easier for her if she hated them, but her love is what brings her back in the end. She could never betray her family. She'll always be on their side even if it makes her life more difficult sometimes, like when the Sabini gang attack her in London because Tommy has been up to mischief. In the end she makes the decision to lump Tommy's activities, even though she might not like them. Ada shrugs it off and decides to get some nice fur coats out of the spoils of gangsterism.

Later on in her story, Ada becomes even more politically minded. Doing so gives her the chance to affect change and a lot of her frustrations come about because she's as smart as Tommy. She's a highly intelligent Shelby, but there's nothing she can do within the family business with that intelligence. But in politics, in that interim period between the two wars, there is a turbulence. A huge period of social, economic and political unrest is taking place and people need change.

The war is so devastating for everyone; people have been decimated. Society has been upended by everything and it was the beginning of the end of the class system. I think politics offers people like Tommy and Ada a chance to get their hands on the country and bring in change. People move between the classes. Upward social mobility is a new thing. If you were born into the lower class you used to stay there your whole life, but the First World War is the end of life as that society knew it and politics offers people the chance to give themselves a new life. For Ada, her family have hacked their way through the jungle

Pol, I'm paid by the company now so I have to talk to other people.

Ada Thorne

and demanded a change in their status through business. Politics is the next natural step for them, which we see at the end of Series Four.

Gangsters became politicians; politicians become gangsters. It was brilliant to be a part of that storyline and I found the politics angle very exciting. It can be so frustrating as a woman when your storyline focuses only on a love affair, or your character getting a shiny new dress. But Ada is a character who's literate, articulate and clued-up. She's able to challenge someone as powerful and fearsome as Tommy with her own personal politics. It eventually has an effect on him and causes him to struggle with the morality of what he's been doing.

Ada offers that narratively, in a way that no other character can. Tommy can't escape the soul-searching when his sister is pushing it upon him. If it were somebody else – an outside character, say – he would find it easy to dismiss that person. He could walk away. But he can't walk away when it's his family: someone like Polly, or Ada. There aren't too many people that wouldn't be afraid of Tommy Shelby, but Ada isn't afraid of him at all.

Peaky Blinders captures the dynamic between a brother and sister so well. And those sibling conversations can be very funny because brothers and sisters hate each other sometimes. The reality is that they love each other and would die for each other, but it's really fun when you see the volatile interactions between Ada and Tommy. I've spoken to Steve about the sibling relationship; the things brothers and sisters do to each other when they're kids. My brother and I tried to kill one another numerous times, but there's a deep love and loyalty there. At the end of the day we can slag our family off until we're blue in the face, but if anyone else tried, we'd eat them alive.

I hope Ada's story ends with her holding power in some way, because she wants to run things without the violence, bloodshed and shady dealings used by the Shelby business. She wants her family to be legitimate in some way. I want her to find status

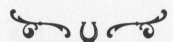

I came back for love. And common sense.

Ada Thorne

– economically and culturally. I'd like to see her intelligence embraced. But I'd hope she sticks with the family. Ada is my favourite and while she is of the new school of business thinking that arrives in *Peaky Blinders*, she is eternally on 'team Tommy'. Though she would hate to admit that.

Ada will forever challenge Tommy, especially if she doesn't think his way of working is necessarily right. But she will also always protect her brother and take care of him. As the story progresses, Tommy comes to Ada more and more. In times of stress, he finds himself near her and there's an interesting dynamic between them that becomes almost maternal, from Ada to Tommy.

I love Ada. She's a badass. The feral princess; one part of Birmingham's royal family. I try to take a little bit of her into my life because I'd like to think that no one would mess with Ada. Any time I'm feeling a bit fearful I'll remember her and what she might do. I even bought a coat this winter that was very Ada Thorne. It had a fancy collar and I thought, *'Why not?'*

We could all do with having a little bit of Ada in us somewhere.

The Confidante

Natasha O'Keeffe on Lizzie Stark

Tommy Shelby is a very careful man. His enemies would love to have inside knowledge of the tricks he pulls and the plans he makes, so in order to survive in his search for power he surrounds himself only with people he can trust implicitly. Lizzie is exactly that character. The pair of them have a mutual understanding: they're both from those Brummie streets, where they ran around the cobbled roads of Small Heath, knock-kneed with bruised legs, as very hungry kids, stealing things from the grocers. Lizzie and Tommy were street urchins. Maybe Tommy has always loved and trusted Lizzie for that very reason.

Later, he uses her, like he uses everybody. As Lizzie grows older and the world treats her unkindly, Lizzie becomes a prostitute – Tommy occasionally sees her for sex. But when his brother John announces he's going to marry Lizzie in Series One, Tommy offers to sleep with her again for no other reason than to test her loyalty to his younger sibling. Lizzie fails. I think like so many characters in the show, she is trying to climb the ladder from the very beginning. Getting into the Shelby family by marriage was certainly one way of doing that, but she ruins her first attempt.

The realization breaks her heart. Lizzie is on the breadline at first, struggling to survive, and prostitution was her way of making some extra cash. When I initially heard about the character, it was only set to be a small role. Lizzie Stark was to have one scene with Tommy – her infamous moment in the car – and as far as Steve Knight was concerned it was initially only meant to be minor part. Before the start of production on Series Two I was surprised to receive a phone call asking if I'd like to come back. I was shocked. 'Er … *Yeah*!' I thought, jumping at the chance.

Like a lot of actresses, I've written a backstory for my character, one that helps me to play the role psychologically. The subtext of Lizzie's relationship with Tommy – something that you won't see in the actual show – is that Tommy has sussed out that she can hold his secrets close; hers too. Meanwhile, Lizzie has seen and experienced things in life that she wishes not to see anymore and, like so many characters in the show, she's desperate to escape. She's come from Birmingham's working-class life, where she was an ambitious creature to begin with.

When we first meet her, she wants to rise to the top and Tommy is her way of getting there. I think there was, and still is, a desire to swim upstream, an urge that's reinforced when Lizzie remembers the doldrums she once lived in. Anything is more glamorous than that and men have treated her far more badly than Tommy ever has, or will. Lizzie knows how bad it can get and she doesn't want to go back. She's a smart girl; she knows

Yes, it can only be yours, the day by the canal when you were fucking somebody else in your head. Except it wasn't her who got pregnant.

Lizzie Stark

what she's doing. Lizzie is always in an element of her own and she's doing business, even at the very beginning.

I think it helps that she's very much in love with Tommy, which we see from the get-go. She's had some moments in the story where she's not been happy with the order of things, especially in Series Four, but she's a loyal one and Tommy exerts his knowledge of that, even when she hates it. From her early introduction, first we see that he has a control over her; he has Lizzie exactly where he wants her. Tommy keeps that up throughout the story. Even by Series Five, when they're married and have had a child together, their power dynamic hasn't really changed. She's become more vocal in their relationship for sure, and he listens to her more closely, but Lizzie always feels she needs to be the first person that gets the information. It really peeves her when she isn't. Tommy's business priorities lay elsewhere.

Before they marry she is often a pawn in his game. One of the heavier moments for Lizzie and Tommy takes place in Series Two, when he asks her to act as if she's going to sleep with Field Marshal Henry Russell in the last episode. Tommy wants him distracted. He plans to take over Darby Sabini's territories at the Epsom racetrack. Meanwhile, Tommy has been forced by Major Chester Campbell and the British government to assassinate Field Marshal Russell, but he is delayed. Lizzie is sexually assaulted by Russell and, when Tommy eventually arrives, he shoots his target dead.

Lizzie is happy to go along with the plan initially because she was never supposed to have sex with Field Marshal Russell, though it says a lot that she would even go that far. That's how desperate she is to stay in the Shelby orbit and to not return to the life she once had. By that stage, she has become Tommy's secretary and life is improving for her. Tommy knows that too, which is why he's able to make his unpleasant request. As far as he's concerned, Lizzie's not going to get up and leave him or the company. It's quite a power to have.

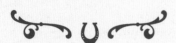

I wish just once you wouldn't pay me. As if we were ordinary people.

Lizzie Stark

That finale of Series Two is the first taste of heightened drama for Lizzie, which brought on an interesting challenge for me. Playing that scene wasn't enjoyable because of its brutal context, but it was powerful and satisfying, and it was impactful. Why? Because there was a heaviness to the story: Lizzie is raped, but it's also a telling indication of just how far she will go for Tommy. There's something sad about how desperate she is to not return to her old life.

Life soon changes for Lizzie. Once she becomes Tommy's secretary, she hears of his really personal matters. That role brings its challenges. In Series Four, before her marriage to Tommy and their child together, it's Christmastime. In one scene, there's a conversational tennis that Tommy and Lizzie play all the time. She's under his nose, but Tommy is talking about a prostitute he's going to sleep with. That kills Lizzie inside, because she does so much for him. I love how Steve writes so many parallels and that moment is a mirroring of the money that is handed to her in the car in Series One, and later when she is asked to lure Field Marshal Henry Russell. But in those moments, when Tommy hands her the money, that's the power – he's saying, 'I'm taking the power from you.'

Lizzie really is interesting. Some writers would make her two-dimensional, where she is either fire or desire for Tommy, but Steve has written her to be much more complex than that. As we know, relationships have so many more layers to them in *Peaky Blinders*. At times, it seems as if she's thinking, *'What the hell am I doing?'* I'm sure she'd love to dive for the exit at times, but the exit isn't very kind for her, either.

Once Tommy and Lizzie become linked romantically, their relationship seems to be for show. They have a baby together when the usual way of settling down in those days would have been to marry first. If you were in a normal relationship, the family would arrive afterwards. But Lizzie and Tommy have done things the opposite way around – there is nothing normal about them. She's had the baby with him and then the marriage takes place

Lizzie: Your brother is ten times the man you are.

Tommy: Of that, I have no doubt.

later, but marriage, when it happens, is a benefit to Tommy. He's a politician: he has a role as the Shelby MD and then he has a wife and a beautiful little girl. For Lizzie, that's a winner, too. *They put a ring on it*. But it's all for show. In Series Five, that issue bubbles to the surface and Tommy becomes a bit more loving and tender as a result.

I respect Lizzie's desire to climb the ladder. She's gone from lady of the night to lady of the manor, and she never seems to give up. I think she's got brains. She uses her nous, intelligence and integrity to get where she is in the story today. And she's got emotional intelligence. There's a blend with Lizzie where she can be a strong creature, but also there's a real softness to her. She can be shot down quite quickly because she's in love with Tommy, and he is probably her biggest weakness.

Tommy seems to be Lizzie's one and only. She knows he could have his way with some of the other female characters in the story. I can't imagine that many men will have treated her well in life; I don't think she knows what that really feels like, so she has nothing to compare it to and her vulnerability shines out all the time. I've always had this theory that Lizzie endured an abusive relationship with her father. It's a backstory I've made for her myself, but in general her relationships with men have been complicated. Lizzie is working with what's she's got and that's to be commended.

It's in those times when Tommy tries to pay Lizzie that her sensitive side comes through: it reminds her of a past she wants to forget. We first get a sense of that in Series Two, when he pays her for sex in his office. She remarks that it would be nice if – just once – he didn't feel the need to do that. Lizzie was a lot younger then and she wants a sense of love and respect from Tommy; she wants to be with him in a relationship sense, rather than having sex with him as a prostitute. I also think it takes us back to the idea of a business-minded Lizzie: there is a love that she needs, but she mainly likes the thought of having a legitimate love and a separate legitimate business, which is why she is so pleased when Tommy later offers her the role of company secretary.

In the final scene of Series Three, the Shelbys have gathered as a family and Tommy gives everyone their cash handouts, what he calls 'The King's Shilling'. This is the reward promised to them at the beginning of the story arc. The money is for the family's future plans and some of them, like Arthur, are going to America; others are told of their next move. But the scene doesn't end well for anyone. Lizzie reacts. When Tommy passes her the money, he's reminding her of her old self, *the old Lizzie*, of what she used to be. The money is thrown back and Tommy praises her loyalty.

'Lizzie, I want it known that on some nights it was you who stopped my heart from breaking. No one else.'

While she doesn't say anything during that scene, she flies up and down emotionally. It hits her hard. There is anger and sorrow.

I've loved playing Lizzie. The fun is in putting on some of the most amazing costumes in drama, particularly those that have come in the last few series. They've been a dream and I've often felt a million dollars on set, especially as she becomes wealthier. The look of Lizzie is so different to what I might wear myself. I'm in jeans and trainers most of the time, so she is such a transformation for me, and with the hair and make-up it's astonishing.

I also like playing a Brummie. When I speak in the accent, a different person takes over. I become friendlier. I'll stop to chat with anyone and, given the chance, I'd probably give sugar to my next-door neighbour on set. I love to be in the vibe of 1920s Small Heath and Birmingham. I feel intimately there and I become that character: *I am Lizzie* – back in the twenties, climbing the ladder, trying to avoid a fictitious past that will forever come back to haunt me.

It's God Who Pulls the Trigger

Vengeance lurks as the Shelby family consider their escape from gangster life.

An Insider's Look at Series Four

Cliffhanger! Arthur, John, Michael and Polly, sentenced to death following Tommy Shelby's political chicanery at the end of Series Three, find themselves approaching the hangman's gallows. As part of a deal struck with Winston Churchill, it's believed the foursome – accused on various charges of murder, sedition and conspiracy to cause explosion – will receive a pardon. On the day of their execution, following two years in jail, however, no such respite has arrived. A question looms over the tense opening of *Peaky Blinders*' fourth chapter: will one or more the show's leading characters die in dramatic fashion?

'From the start, the Peaky Blinders are in bad shape,' says Series Four director, David Caffrey. 'In the script, Steven Knight gave us a big, powerful, impactful opening. It's interesting, what you have to do as a director in that situation. I realized the audience would understand that if this lot all hanged then the show was pretty much over. But how do you sell it in such a way that you can save the characters and still make the story dramatic and powerful, and have the hairs on people's necks stand up?

'As we learned from David Chase (writer and producer of HBO drama, *The Sopranos*), any major character can be killed, and at any time. So, when you watch the very end of *The Sopranos* – it was the final scene of the final episode – of course Tony is going to get whacked … isn't he? The whole build-up, with different people – potential assassins – coming in and out of the diner, created tension, then nothing happens and the screen goes to black. Let the audience decide. (Or, on the other hand, they might have had a film option and had to leave it ambiguous.)

'At the end of the day, we're dramatists. We want people to be shocked, in order to really make the drama strong. For the opening of Series Four in *Peaky Blinders*, we followed the methods of director Otto Bathurst (Series One: episodes one, two and three) and his team and built as much tension as we could in the way the actors performed and how we photographed everything, and then the way we arranged the music. That was an original track sung and performed by our genius composers Antony Genn and Martin Slattery.'

> **I hear you dress well, Mr Shelby. But now I see, not so well as me.**
>
> — Luca Changretta

At the very last moment, and with the hangman's rope already fastened around their necks, a series of political pardons are granted by the king's private secretary. But the Peaky Blinders are immediately faced with another mortal threat: the Changrettas, an

Italian crime family. Enraged at the murders of Vicente and Angel Changretta in Series Three, the New York Mafia have dispatched a crew of assassins to wreak vengeance on the Peaky Blinders. Each member of Tommy Shelby's gang is sent a Christmas card with an ominous black hand printed inside – the notification of a Mob vendetta. 'Those black-hand calling cards actually existed,' says Caffrey. 'I thought they were a device that Steve had made up for dramatic purposes, but we saw several examples of real black-hand vendetta cards from the period.'

Revenge is in the air

Tommy's paranoia is heightened from the opening episode. Having discovered that two members of his domestic staff are Italian, he then learns of their plot to kill him on Christmas Day. As with all incidents of violence within the theatre of *Peaky Blinders*, Tommy's past has drawn a terrifying reality to those closest to him. 'Every series has a mind-altering theme,' says Steven Knight of Series Four. 'The first one was postwar anger, the second was cocaine and the third one was opium. The fourth is about revenge.'

This plotline brings into play two chillingly violent individuals: Tommy Shelby, leader of the Peaky Blinders and a man ravaged both by the loss of his wife and the threats to his son, Charlie, in Series Three. The other is Luca Changretta, member of the New York Mafia and son of the deceased Vicente, played by Adrien Brody. Luca strikes first.

> # There is no rest for me in this world; maybe in the next.
>
> ## – Tommy Shelby

In a heavy opening episode, John Shelby is murdered by Changretta's hitmen, who launch a machine-gun assault on his family home. Michael is standing alongside him when the assassination takes place. He is seriously injured in the hit, but survives. By episode two, with the Changretta feud claiming its first victims, Tommy and Luca meet, head-to-head

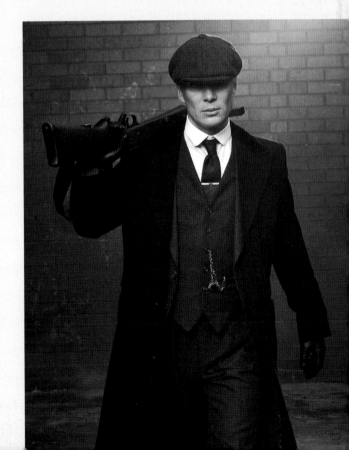

in a confrontation during which the Italian unveils his plans to murder the entire Peaky Blinders family. His intention is for Tommy to survive until the bitter end, so he can suffer the pain of both intense grief and remorse.

'Series Four is a full-on gang war,' says David Caffrey. 'If you're a director and you get people like Cillian and Adrien, it's an amazing opportunity. Those two actors set their stall out in the beginning in that brilliant scene, the first meeting, with Tommy at one end of the room, Luca the other. There was a phenomenal gameplay between the two, both in the script and how they performed.

'The scene is where Luca lines up several bullets to represent which gang member he was going to kill. There was a Peaky name etched on each one. I wanted Luca to flick one at Cillian. With CGI I was going to send it the twenty feet or so towards him, the tip spinning then stopping and finally pointing at Tommy. That's nigh on impossible to shoot for real. I said to Adrien, "Just do the flick part and we'll do the rest in post production …" But in the last take, Adrien flicked the bullet at Cillian, it curled like a banana the whole way down the long table and stopped right in front of him, spinning before pointing directly at Tommy. It actually happened. You could've attempted that a million times and it wouldn't have happened so perfectly, it was one of a string of good fortunes we had on Series Four.'

A little help from his friends

With the walls closing in on the Peaky Blinders, Tommy enlists the help of his friends, the Lees. Aberama Gold, a Gypsy hitman regarded even by the gang as being a savage, is also called in as extra protection. Played by Aidan Gillen, Gold's payment for helping out the gang is business representation for his son, Bonnie (Jack Rowan) – a powerful boxer with a promising career as a heavyweight. In his next fight, Bonnie proves his worth by knocking out the former champion, Billy Mills. The Peaky Blinders immediately sign him up, sensing a lucrative partnership.

Aberama's introduction to the show is both memorable and bloody: he stabs an assassin preparing to make another hit at John Shelby's funeral. This gory entrance was deliberate, explains Caffrey, establishing a brutal ruthlessness to a character offset by a dapper suit and trilby hat.

'We thought, to counterbalance his appearance we should give him a really strong, visceral and violent entrance. So when he rocks up and kills one of the Italians, it was pretty

heavy duty. Just that combination of him and his son, Bonnie, was interesting for the viewer. Bonnie doesn't bat an eyelid when his dad stabs someone in the chest forty times. That told the audience everything they needed to know about Aberama and Bonnie Gold.'

Aberama later helps Polly and Michael Gray to evade the Changrettas' reach, and the duo (one which Helen McCrory describes as 'the King and Queen of the Gypsies') form a formidable union. When Aberama kisses Polly during a romantic riverside picnic, she adds a frisson of danger to their tryst by pulling out a knife and pressing it to his windpipe.

'That was one of those scenes where you get lucky,' says Caffrey. 'We had two brilliant actors, but were a bit stuck. We had to do the scene quickly and the location by the river wasn't exactly where I'd wanted to film, but we got them by a little stretch of water with a fire going and they were cooking something Aberama had caught. The actors made that scene what it was and really made something of the relationship between them. I'll be interested to see where they go with those two in the future … Aberama Gold, the Gypsy hitman: *how does Steve Knight come up with names like that?*'

The unravelling

The Peaky Blinders' unravelling, a process that begins in Series Three, is complicated even further. With the family's security threatened, Tommy brazenly uses the funeral of his brother as a trap to expose the Changretta assassins. Arthur is devastated by the murder of John,

promising to avenge his death by killing Luca; Arthur's wife, Linda, eventually convinces him to back away from the dark burden.

For Polly, the emotional fallout weighs heavily, too. Having escaped criminal execution, she lays the blame for her near death with Tommy. Self-medicating her mental anguish with booze and pills in a psychological breakdown, she begins to hear voices, while experiencing a series of haunting visions. To prepare for Polly's tumult, Helen McCrory turned to the American illusionist David Blaine for advice.

'I talked to him about seances, mind tricks, voices, all this kind of stuff,' she says. 'He was lovely. I'd met him through a friend. He was very generous with his time and gave me lots of books. He talked about the subject to me like a historian. He studies; he has papers from hundreds of years ago, and the works of people that have written about it.

'It was fascinating. He had a library full of stories. He said to me, "You think you hear voices for three reasons. One: *you do hear voices*, and you are what we would call psychotic, paranoid, or schizophrenic. Secondly: you're pretending to hear them to make money (such as a fraudster posing as a fortune-teller, or a psychic, as Polly experiences in Series Two). Thirdly: it's a suggestion placed there by someone else." Polly is influenced by suggestion at the seance in Series Two. That someone could abuse her in that way, and abuse people's wants and hopes and dreams and grief, is just terrible.

'In Series Four, Polly starts living somewhere between life and death. She has psychotic episodes for weeks and months. As it's gone on, she's not able to cope and she loses herself to morphine, cocaine and whisky, living in a twilight zone where she's talking to old ghosts and living in the past. I also went to occult bookshops and talked to people there about the subject, as well as Gypsy traditions.

'Polly is such an old soul that she absolutely believes in all of that stuff. She talks to spirits and she feels people's energies. I think everybody understands that idea because even if you don't think you're sensitive, everybody has a sense. It's the basic reason why sometimes we walk into pub and meet two people: one we'll absolutely get on with; the other will make us feel fucking weird and we really don't like them. They might be fine but there's a gut instinct. Everyone understands that feeling, we all have that, but Polly has it turned up to a hundred.'

Polly strikes a deal with Luca Changretta: in exchange for his sparing the surviving Shelby family members, and Michael, she must help him during the vendetta with Tommy. But in an unexpected twist, Polly's union with the Changrettas is revealed to have been a ruse all along, the plot devised by Polly and Tommy. (This detail is not imparted to Michael, though; he is happy to go along with the betrayal plot to save Polly.) The mobster eventually takes a swing at the Peaky Blinders when Bonnie Gold fights Goliath – a heavyweight boxer and nephew of London gangster and

Peaky Blinders associate, Alfie Solomons. As the bout is contested, Arthur is seemingly murdered behind the scenes. When the Peaky Blinders reach out to Al Capone – a rival to Luca's New York mob – the upper hand is transferred to Birmingham. The remaining Changretta men, none of them blood-related to their head member, switch loyalties, leaving him exposed. Luca faces down Tommy. But Arthur, having faked his own death, emerges from the shadows to strike, avenging John in a bloody end to a murderous vendetta.

When you're dead already, you're free.

– Polly Gray

There is yet another betrayal to uncover. It is discovered that Tommy was served up by Alfie Solomons, who provided Luca's gang with the opportunity to strike at the Peaky Blinders during the heavyweight showdown between Bonnie and Goliath. When Tommy eventually locates Alfie, it's revealed that he is dying from cancer. Desperately, Alfie orders a hesitant Tommy to kill him, forcing him into the task by firing first. A swift return shot to the head ends Alfie's story in a bleak confrontation.

'Steve only decided to do that scene a day before we filmed it,' says David Caffrey. 'We didn't even know we were going to a beach.

The next day our production circus travelled to Formby in Liverpool; nothing was planned, but the crew were amazing. We got a filming crane on the beach to film for the high, wide shots of Alfie, as Tommy walks away.

'Tom Hardy and Cillian pretty much worked that scene out themselves. They were the ones who decided to pull the guns out and shoot each other at (nearly) the same time. The dialogue was per script, but the two of them shouting at each other and pulling the guns out? They figured that out themselves.

'My cameraman, Cathal Watters (ASC), picked some beautiful shots. He charged off down the beach to find a suitable position. I originally wanted us to be in the water, looking back at both of them. That would have been quite evocative, but we couldn't do it. The tide had gone, but instead he found a stretch of water that made us feel like we *were* watching from the sea. That was a scene that came together very quickly and everyone had to man the pumps to do it, but a lot of hard work and good thinking from the team made it magnificent.'

Tommy Shelby is going to stop the revolution with his cock.

– Ada Thorne

The next chapter

The backdrop to *Peaky Blinders'* next instalment is established throughout the fourth series. Michael and Ada are dispatched to America to establish the New York wing of the Shelby's business interests. 'Ada gets a fabulous new wardrobe,' says Sophie Rundle. 'She's spent so long rejecting that, trying to run away from the spoils of gangster life and distancing herself from the Shelbys. But when she goes to America it offers her a freedom she's always craved. She gets to be a woman out there on her own. Ada out of context of the Shelbys? I'd imagine she's absolutely terrifying.'

Meanwhile, Tommy meets with union provocateur, Jessie Eden, in order to gather intelligence on the Italian gang on his trail; she calls for his help when fighting to improve the pay of workers employed in his factory. Their connection later inspires Tommy to transport himself into the world of politics. By the series' close, Tommy is a Member of Parliament and a father once more, his partner, Lizzie Stark, having fallen pregnant.

The casting of Aidan Gillen

SHAHEEN BAIG: Aberama is shifty. There's nearly always something really shifty about Aidan's characters but, in a similar style to Sam Neill, Aidan has humour, charm and danger, delivered with a wink and a smile. And if someone is utterly charming they can persuade you to do anything.

Aidan's storyline with Helen was an absolute joy. It's really sexy; it felt like she had met her match. His chemistry with Helen came into my thinking when casting. She's so strong, you have to match her – we had to find somebody that could go up against her. Polly is no fool, so you've got to put somebody up against her that you believe she will be attracted to and compelled by. Aidan worked perfectly.

The excesses of the 1920s

STEVEN KNIGHT: During the 1920s, cocaine came into the story. It was legal then, and after the war there was an initial shock when everybody returned home. People were stunned and shell-shocked. Then they thought, 'Fuck this,' and all went mad on alcohol and cocaine. That was the beginning of the roaring twenties, which featured the imagery we see in Hollywood movies, which was all fun and harmless on the surface, with people doing the Charleston at high-end parties.

But that vibe was about everybody not caring. Even the class barriers stopped, people just didn't care. The thing we forget about sending the troops over to France was the officer class had it the worst because they led troops over the top in battles. The officer class was absolutely decimated: half the men were dead and the ones that returned home alive would go out to the pub armed with a revolver.

There was a hedonism that continued until the Wall Street Crash of 1929. That was the beginning of a hangover. The twenties was the binge, and the depression in the thirties was the comedown. It was a very interesting time for our people to be in.

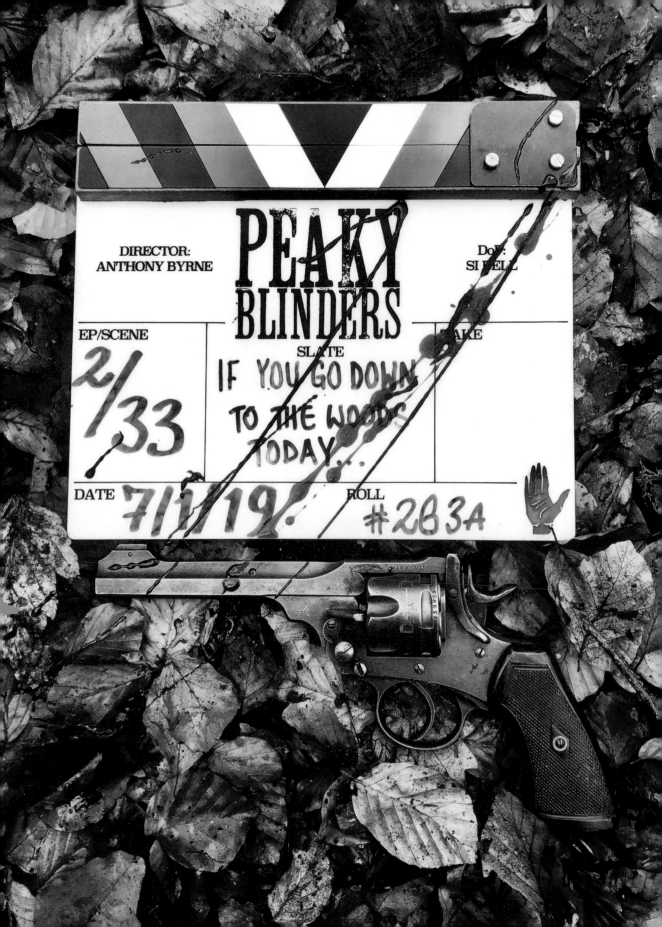

Epilogue: What's Next for Tommy?

By Jamie Glazebrook, Executive Producer

An Insider's Look at Series Five

It's been ten years since Steve, Caryn and I first went to the BBC with Steve's idea for *Peaky Blinders*. His fantasy world of grand mythic narrative woven through historical fact caught the imagination of everyone who heard it. It's been a privilege to share Steve's vision with the wider world, and to see a burgeoning body of fans consume each chapter with so much passion and intelligence.

One of the joys of a returning series like this is that the lead character's experiences become the viewers' experiences. So while in real life none of us, I hope, could ever actually *be* Tommy Shelby, when we watch the episodes we somehow feel that we *are* him. Part of Steve's magic is to marry that complicity with a morality tale made from poetry, politics, secret history, social satire, deep character work, genre thrills, sex, violence and rock 'n' roll. It's boundless.

Another joy is that just as Tommy Shelby's world broadens with each series, it also deepens. Series Five is no exception, and I

believe that Tommy's story has been building to this point ever since we first met him. Facing up to the evil in the world and the despair in his heart, he is compelled to make a choice.

How could these profoundly disturbing themes be wrapped up in such an entertaining, colourful, wild hour of television? Breathing new life into our world, Series Five director Anthony Byrne makes us feel Tommy's predicaments more deeply than ever. His take on the *Peaky Blinders* world is burnished, visceral, witty and soulful.

Some of the show's best moments have been when Tommy's identity and values are challenged – whether that's Princess Tatiana schooling him on how to be an aristocrat, Alfie Solomons calling out his hypocrisy, or Jessie Eden reminding him that he used to believe in things. And the events of Series Five, which include the rise of fascism within the UK, are most certainly challenging …

Having witnessed our characters endeavour to cope with the many aftershocks of the Great War, it's terrifying to feel the tremors of the next world conflict. Steve's already talking about where the story goes from here. I can't tell you anything, of course, but I can say that his ability to surprise, to go deep with Tommy Shelby, and to reinvent *Peaky Blinders*, will never cease to astonish.

First published in Great Britain in 2019 by
Michael O'Mara Books Limited
9 Lion Yard
Tremadoc Road
London SW4 7NQ

A CIP catalogue record for this book is available from the British Library.

Papers used by Michael O'Mara Books Limited are natural, recyclable
products made from wood grown in sustainable forests. The manufacturing
processes conform to the environmental regulations of the country of origin.

Photos © Caryn Mandabach Productions Limited.
Photography by Robert Viglasky and by Matt Squires.
Some behind-the-scenes photography by the crew.

Select image credits: Page 8: John Loveridge; Page 10 © Brian McDonald,
author of *Gangs of London*; Page 11: West Midlands Museum

Every reasonable effort has been made to acknowledge all copyright holders.
Any errors or omissions that may have occurred are inadvertent, and anyone
with any copyright queries is invited to write to the publisher, so that a full
acknowledgement may be included in subsequent editions of this work.

ISBN: 978-1-78929-165-0 in hardback print format
ISBN: 978-1-78929-170-4 in ebook format

2 3 4 5 6 7 8 9 10

Designed by www.us-now.com
Printed and bound in Germany

www.mombooks.com